# Reading
# Techniques

## Revised Edition

Previously published by Georgian Press

Clare West

CAMBRIDGE UNIVERSITY PRESS
Cambridge, New York, Melbourne, Madrid, Cape Town, Singapore,
São Paulo, Delhi, Dubai, Tokyo, Mexico City

Cambridge University Press
The Edinburgh Building, Cambridge CB2 8RU, UK

www.cambridge.org
Information on this title: www.cambridge.org/9780521140706

First published by Georgian Press (Jersey) Limited 1997 as Reading Techniques for FCE
Second edition 2008
Reprinted and published by Cambridge University Press 2010
Reprinted 2011

Printed in the United Kingdom by Latimer Trend

*A catalogue record for this publication is available from the British Library*

ISBN 978-0-521-14070-6 Paperback

Cambridge University Press has no responsibility for the persistence or
accuracy of URLs for external or third-party internet websites referred to in
this publication, and does not guarantee that any content on such websites is,
or will remain, accurate or appropriate. Information regarding prices, travel
timetables and other factual information given in this work is correct at
the time of first printing but Cambridge University Press does not guarantee
the accuracy of such information thereafter.

Produced by AMR Design Ltd (www.amrdesign.com)

## Acknowledgements

The authors and publishers acknowledge the following sources of copyright material and are grateful for the permissions granted. While every effort has been made, it has not always been possible to identify the sources of all the material used, or to trace all copyright holders. If any omissions are brought to our notice we will be happy to include the appropriate acknowledgement on reprinting.

Pages 26, 34 and 38: Extracts from 'Volunteers for a leisure America', 'Waiting game is strictly for pros' and 'TV exposure damages children's speech' from *The Guardian Weekly*, by permission of *The Guardian*.

Pages 32, 54 and 94: Extracts from 'Thieves cut off in their crime', 'Is life really just a game of chance?' and 'Amazing life of the old man of the sea' from *The Daily Mail*, by permission of Solo Syndication. © Daily Mail/Solo Syndication.

Page 46: Extract from *The Seven Wonders of the Ancient World* by Hugh Gethin and Judith Brown (Georgian Press, 1994). © Hugh Gethin and Judith Brown 1994.

Page 56: Extract from *My Early Life* by Winston Churchill (Hamlyn, 1930), by permission of HarperCollins Publishers Limited.

Page 58: Extract from *Adventures in Two Worlds* by A.J. Cronin (Gollancz, 1952), by permission of A.M. Heath & Co. Limited. © A.J. Cronin.

Page 64: 'The Village That Vanished' from *World of Strange Phenomena Omnibus* by Charles Berlitz (Warner Books, 1995).

Page 83: Adapted extracts from the Empire State Building information brochure, by permission of Helmsley-Spear, Inc.

Page 86: Extract from *Friends, Lovers, Chocolate* by Alexander McCall Smith (Little, Brown), by permission of David Higham Associates Limited. © Alexander McCall Smith 2005.

Page 88: Adapted extract from *George Fisher Update*, by permission of George Fisher Limited.

Page 92: Extract from *Sour Sweet* by Timothy Mo, by permission of Andre Deutsch Limited. © Timothy Mo 1982.

Page 98: Adapted article 'My kind of day' by Sue Lloyd-Roberts from *Radio Times*, by permission of BBC Worldwide Limited.

Page 100: Extract from 'Work till you drop' from *The Guardian*, by permission.

Page 103: Adapted extracts from 'London in winter' by Robin Mead, from *20:20*, the West Coast InterCity magazine Dec 1995/Jan 1996, by permission of the author. © Robin Mead 1995.

Page 106: Extract from *As I Walked Out One Midsummer Morning* by Laurie Lee (Penguin Books, 1971), by permission of Penguin Books Limited. © Laurie Lee 1969.

Page 108: The adapted article 'The Real Venice' from *National Geographic*, Oct 1995.

**Photographs** by permission of Roy Rainford/Robert Harding World Imagery/Corbis (page 22); Roger Ressmeyer/Corbis (page 46); Ray Sulgan/Corbis (page 83); Roger Antrobus/Corbis (page 89); Richard Bryant/Arcaid/Corbis (page 101); Adam Woolfill/Corbis (page 103); Pawel Libera/Corbis (page 104); Hans Georg Roth/Corbis (page 109); Douglas Pearson/Corbis (page 112).

Cover image: © Shutterstock

# Contents

# Introduction

Reading in a foreign or second or third language is much more difficult than reading in your mother tongue. It doesn't come naturally and needs a lot of practice. In addition, there are a number of skills and strategies which we use when reading in our first language, without being aware of them. This book identifies and demonstrates these practical skills, and then shows how they can be used in various types of reading tasks. Using the appropriate reading techniques helps people to become much more effective readers, and to tackle examination papers with greater confidence.

## Who is this book for?

*Reading Techniques* is for students at upper-intermediate level who wish to improve their general reading skills in English and/or work specifically towards international exams at B2 level (Common European Framework). It can be used to supplement any coursebook at this level, and is suitable for classroom use, for homework, or for self-study.

## What does *Reading Techniques* offer?

- coverage of the main reading skills required at this level – *skimming, scanning, intensive reading, reading between the lines, speed reading* and *identifying topic, source and register*
- extensive practice in using the skills to deal with three common task types – *multiple choice, gapped texts* and *multiple matching*
- graded texts and tasks
- study boxes with clear step-by-step guidance and regular reminders of the particular skills required
- icons representing skills, to aid visual intelligence
- texts from a wide range of sources, in varying styles and registers
- four full-length practice reading tests.

## How is the book organised?

It is divided into five distinct sections:

### Section 1: Reading Skills

Six important reading skills are presented in this section, with graded practice tasks. There are also three practice units, each practising the skills presented in the previous two units.

### Section 2: Multiple Choice

Five units give guidance and practice in dealing with this traditional but challenging task type. The focus is mainly on opinion, gist, attitude and deducing meaning, but also on detail and features of text organisation.

### Section 3: Gapped Texts

Five units deal with this more recently established task type. Here the focus is on text structure, cohesion and coherence.

### Section 4: Multiple Matching

Five units cover this task type, which can be based on a wide range of texts. The focus is on specific information, details, opinion and attitude.

### Section 5: Practice Tests

There are four tests, of three parts each, with full-length texts and tasks appropriate to the level and specifications of the FCE examination.

## How should *Reading Techniques* be used?

Section 1 should be studied first, because this section describes the reading skills and how to use them. Sections 2 – 4 can be studied in any order. However, as the tasks and texts have been carefully selected and graded for level, it is important to work through each section from its first unit to its last. Section 5 should be done at the end.

## Tips for the student

- Make sure you really understand Section 1 before you move on to other sections.

- Memorise the icons – they are there to help you remember which skills to use.

| | | |
|---|---|---|
| skimming | | reading between the lines |
| scanning | | speed reading |
| intensive reading | | topic, source and register |

- Use a pencil to complete the tasks the first time, in case you want to go back and try again later.

- Check your answers for each unit before you move on.

- Practise your reading on whatever you enjoy – newspapers, magazines, short stories, emails, blogs, websites and so on.

## Finally . . .

If reading skills are practised often enough, they become almost instinctive, and then reading itself becomes a natural, pleasurable activity. I hope that the techniques in this book will make reading easier and therefore more enjoyable for everyone.

*Clare West*

# Glossary

You will find these terms used throughout the book. They are all connected in some way with reading skills.

**gapped text**                a task in which you read a text with gaps in it, then choose which sentences should fit in the gaps

**gist**                the main point(s) or general meaning of a text or part of a text

**intensive reading**         the skill of reading carefully and thoroughly, so that you understand as much as possible about a text

**multiple choice**         a task in which you answer questions about a text by choosing the correct answer from several options

**multiple matching**       a task in which you scan a text or texts to find specific information to match a set of questions

**narrator**            the person who is telling a story

**reading between the lines**  the skill of deducing meaning from context, and gaining a deeper understanding of what the writer is implying

**register**            the style of language suitable for a particular use (e.g. formal, informal, neutral)

**scanning**            the skill of reading quickly in order to find some specific detailed information

**skimming**            the skill of reading quickly in order to find out what the main points of a text are

**source**              where a text comes from (e.g. newspaper, novel, diary)

**speed reading**        the skill of reading quickly while finding out the gist of a text

**topic**              the subject of a text (e.g. shopping, money, travel)

# Reading Skills

# Unit 1

# Skimming

> If you want to know roughly what a text is about, you read it through quickly
> – this is **skimming**. You let your eye run over it, rather like throwing a flat stone
> onto a lake, so that it just skims the surface. Then you should have **the gist**
> – that is, the general meaning without any of the details.

**A** Look quickly at this short text and say briefly what it is about, in your own words, in one sentence. Do not read every word. Use the guidance to help you.

> I usually went by bus, but sometimes if I wanted to save my bus fare for some project or other, I walked instead. Of course, this took much longer, but I followed the bus route, all the way down Dyke Road to the shops at the roundabout, and then heading down Montpelier Road towards the sea, past the townhouses with their neat window boxes, St Michael's church with its tall spire, and the solid, well-built Lloyds Bank building on the corner, until I reached the school.

**GUIDANCE**   What tense should you use?

**B** Do the same with this text.

> It seems that most of us want more holidays than we actually get, apart from a small number of workaholics who do not take all the days off they are entitled to. It is important, however, according to the experts, to make sure that you use your time off sensibly, to relax and unwind from the pressures of the daily routine. Some holidays can be more exhausting than work, so it is crucial to plan the kind of holiday that is appropriate for your personal needs.

**GUIDANCE**
1 What is the topic, in one word?
2 What advice is being given?
3 What does 'crucial' mean?

C Write one sentence giving the gist of this text.

The old woman looked at the pale faces under the umbrellas and sniffed scornfully. In her day, they hadn't worried about the hole in the ozone layer. Well, there probably hadn't been one then. She remembered slapping coconut oil on and lying on the beach, sizzling almost, in the baking sun. Now it was barrier cream, Factor 30, and sunhats all the time. 'And we used to eat whatever we fancied, too,' she thought. 'It never did us any harm.' Things weren't what they used to be.

GUIDANCE          What are the two times or periods mentioned?

D Do the same with this text.

The expansion of tourist development in Spain has brought about a decline in long-established agricultural methods. Young people are no longer prepared to tend the olives and the vines, when higher wages are being offered by the construction and service industries.

GUIDANCE          1 Can you think of an adjective that describes a long-established custom, beginning with **t**?
                  2 Which tenses are used in this text?
                  3 Ask yourself – What is happening? Where? Why?

E Do the same with this text.

A shortage of rainfall in parts of Europe has meant restrictions on water consumption for many residents and, consequently, greater interest in the conservation of what is, after all, one of our most valuable resources. Water companies are investing considerable amounts in the maintenance and improvement of their reservoirs and pipework, and many individual consumers now collect rainwater for their gardens in water butts and tanks.

GUIDANCE          1 Don't worry about vocabulary details like 'reservoirs' and 'butts'.
                  2 Find another word or expression for 'shortage of rainfall'.
                  3 Ask yourself – What has happened? Where? Why? What is the result?

F Write one sentence giving the gist of this text.

## A CITY ON THE MOVE

Every year, air pollution in the capital is at its worst during holiday weekends – especially in July, when most people leave by car for their holiday destination, and at the end of 5 August, when they return. To combat this, new transport measures are being introduced by the authorities, including the building of a new tram line for the south of the city, a ban on Sunday traffic in several 10 streets, and an ambitious plan for 56 km of cycle tracks and new pedestrian zones.

There has even been a proposal, supported by the mayor, that public transport should be free on days when pollution reaches a dangerous level; ozone readings would be 15 taken and public announcements would be made on radio and television, to let people know. Not only are the authorities trying to prevent the chaos caused by public transport strikes in the past, they also want to be able 20 to guarantee safe air for everyone.

GUIDANCE

1 What do 'combat', 'measures' and 'guarantee' mean?
2 When is this problem 'at its worst'?
3 Is this text mainly about public transport, or air pollution? Look at the beginning and end of the text.

G Write one sentence giving the gist of this text.

## SPEED CAMERAS

More and more speed cameras are being installed on Britain's roads in order to bring down the number of serious accidents and make motorists aware of the dangers of 5 driving too fast. The police, who are backing this move, are in favour of making the cameras highly visible – many of them are placed in bright yellow boxes, so that drivers can see them from a distance and slow down.

10 However, recent research in New Zealand appears to run counter to these initiatives. Officials at the Land Transport Safety

Authority in Wellington discovered that hidden cameras were actually more effective than visible ones in reducing driving speeds 15 on all roads. Although drivers were not able to see the cameras, warning signs indicated the start of the speed camera zone, and it seems likely that motorists drove more cautiously overall because they did not know the exact 20 location of the cameras. Overt cameras, on the other hand, had only a localised effect, by reducing actual accidents on the few metres of road covered by the camera.

GUIDANCE

1 What does the research show?
2 Which two things are being compared in the text?

**H** Write one sentence giving the gist of this text.

## CLEAN KIDS

Some scientists think that parents make too big a fuss about hygiene, and that daily contact with bacteria and viruses can be good for youngsters. A recent study conducted by the University Children's Hospital in Munich showed that children who had at least two mild virus infections before their first birthday were only half as likely to be diagnosed with asthma or related allergies when they were seven, compared with children who had been ill only once or not at all. This finding supports the hypothesis that today's ultra-clean lifestyle is the reason for an increase in allergies in the general population in developed countries. It is possible, although this is not yet established, that contact with the bacteria in soil and water is needed for cells in human immune systems to develop correctly. So parents should not overreact if their children sometimes get muddy or dirty when playing outside.

**GUIDANCE**

1 What does the research show?
2 What is the advice to parents?

**I** Write one sentence giving the gist of this text. It is not necessary to list all the suggestions in the article.

## A BETTER NIGHT'S SLEEP

Many people complain of sleeping badly at night. There is no single reliable cure for insomnia, but instead of just taking sleeping pills, sufferers should attempt to find the root cause of the problem and tackle that.

Let's look at some of the most common causes of insomnia. Worrying about some aspect of your life or work can often prevent you from sleeping. Try to calm your anxieties before you go to bed, and if you wake up with something on your mind, get up and sort it out if you can.

Another frequent problem is overexcitement of the nervous system. All substances containing caffeine can induce sleeplessness, so try to avoid alcohol, coffee, tea, etc. too near bedtime. Parties and other late-night activities can also overstimulate and cause insomnia.

Finally, a few tips to make sure you are as comfortable as possible. Check that your bed does not need replacing; you'll probably need to buy a new one every ten years or so. Keep the bedroom temperature cool: heat will prevent you from sleeping. Read for a while if you find that helpful. Above all, try to maintain a happy frame of mind – if you dread going to bed, you'll find it more difficult to get to sleep. If you bear all these points in mind, I'm sure you'll achieve a healthy, normal sleep pattern in time.

**GUIDANCE**

1 What is the problem?
2 What is the main aim of the article?

# Unit
# 2 Scanning

**Scanning** is a reading technique used only when you need to find answers to specific questions. Often the answers are short and factual, and may be numbers or names. If the text is long, you may not have time to read all of it in order to find your answers. Look carefully at the questions first, decide which general topic they refer to, then let your eye run over the text until it is caught by a relevant section or paragraph. Concentrate on this section only, to find the answers.

**A** Match the questions (1 – 10) to the newspaper advertisement categories (A – H). You will need to use some letters more than once.

**1** Where could children spend the summer?

**2** Which company offers the cheapest flights to Vancouver?

**3** Where can you watch young acrobats?

**4** Where can you see some traditional dancing?

**5** Which new release is about a performer's assistant?

**6** Where can you sample different types of food?

**7** Which company offers boating trips?

**8** Where can you buy traditional roses?

**9** Who would like to meet a girl who is interested in music?

**10** Where can you buy old necklaces, earrings, etc?

| | | | |
|---|---|---|---|
| **A** airfares | **B** fairs and shows | **C** holidays | **D** music festivals |
| **E** films | **F** personal | **G** gardening | **H** do-it-yourself |

**B** Now answer the 10 questions above by scanning the advertisements for the answers.

## THE LATEST FILMS

**BLUE IN THE FACE (15)**
Stories and jokes about Brooklyn life. Indulgent companion piece to *Smoke*, with Harvey Keitel, Roseanne, and many cameos. Director: Wayne Wang.
*Renoir* (020 8837 8402)   *Richmond* (020 8332 0030)
*Ritzy* (020 7737 2121)

**ROUGH MAGIC (12)**
Magician's assistant Bridget Fonda finds true magic in Mexico. Engaging oddity from director Clare Peploe. With Russell Crowe.
*Odeons: Haymarket, Kensington, Swiss Cottage*
0870 505 0007

## LEISURE ACTIVITIES

**PARENTS** Are your children bored during the holidays? Camp Beaumont – day & residential camps. Brochure 0171 724 2233

### HOSEASONS
#### FOR BRITAIN'S BEST BOATING
*There is still time to book your boating holidays on all Britain's finest waterways. Including Norfolk Broads, canals, Thames, Cambs and Scotland. Short breaks too! Quote B2329.*
**FREEPHONE 0800 520 520**

**RED ROSE COTTAGES** Super self-catering in Forest of Bowland & Lancashire. Explore pretty villages, countryside, heritage & coast. 0845 273105

## FAIRS AND SHOWS

**LONDON**
**Adams Antiques Fair**
Ideal opportunity to see and buy silver, jewellery, glass, porcelain, furniture and other decorative items.
*Royal Horticultural Society Halls*, Greycoat Street, SW1 (020 7834 4333). Tomorrow, 9.30am–4.30pm; £6.

**BELFAST**
**Ballysillan Carnival Day**
Featuring stalls, demonstrations and activities for all the family.
*Ballysillan Leisure Centre* (02890 391040). Today, midday–6pm; admission free.

**BRIGHTON**
**Chinese State Circus**
Famous circus returns with some spellbinding action that includes 14 boys balancing on one bicycle.
*The Big Top,* Preston Park (01273 709709). Today, tomorrow; times vary; adults £10, children £4.

**HEREFORD**
**Annual Festival of Scottish Dance**
Enjoy a spectacular weekend of demonstrations and performances.
*Wyeside Arts Centre*, Castle Street (01432 552555). Today, tomorrow, times vary; telephone for details.

**HALIFAX**
**UNICEF Music Day**
Charity celebration with a range of musical events.
*Piece Hall* (01422 358086). Tomorrow, midday–3pm; free.

**MAIDSTONE**
**Festival of English Food and Wine**
Family entertainment including stalls, demonstrations and puppet shows. Also wine tasting and food tasting and, on Sunday only, a presentation by the celebrity television chef Michael Barry.
*Leeds Castle* (01622 880 008). Today, tomorrow, 10am–5pm; £8, children £3.

## AIRFARES

### Canada

From Gatwick, Manchester, East Midlands, Glasgow

| | |
|---|---|
| TORONTO | £269 |
| MONTREAL | £269 |
| HALIFAX | £319 |
| WINNIPEG | £349 |
| VANCOUVER | £349 |
| CALGARY | £349 |
| EDMONTON | £349 |

Canadian Affair ATOL 3971
589 Fulham Road London SW6 5UA

**020 7385 4400**

### CURRENT BEST BUYS ON THE WORLD'S FINEST AIRLINES

| (excl. taxes) | one way | return from | | one way | return from |
|---|---|---|---|---|---|
| SYDNEY | £429 | £569 | NEW YORK | £215 | £275 |
| PERTH | £414 | £644 | BOSTON | £229 | £299 |
| AUCKLAND | £452 | £715 | FLORIDA | £259 | £369 |
| BANGKOK | £298 | £484 | LOS ANGELES | £295 | £339 |
| HONG KONG | £337 | £484 | SAN FRANCISCO | £295 | £371 |
| SINGAPORE | £325 | £484 | TORONTO | £238 | £334 |
| BALI | £364 | £539 | VANCOUVER | £355 | £425 |
| SAIGON | £397 | £595 | CARIBBEAN | £275 | £434 |
| TOKYO | £386 | £745 | MEXICO CITY | £353 | £452 |
| DELHI | £311 | £441 | KATHMANDU | £365 | £573 |

*Trailfinders*   194 Kensington High Street, London W8 7RG
020 7938 3939   www.trailfinders.com

## PERSONAL

ORIENTAL LADY, 30s, tall, elegant, attractive, brainy, well educated, professional, seeks compatible gentleman. London. Box 1299.

FARMER, 40, seeks good-looking girl who enjoys countryside and classical music. Midlands. Box 2199.

ATTRACTIVE MALE, 36, fun loving, successful, sporty, great sense of humour, seeks Miss Right. Photo please. Box 0999.

## GARDENING

Old-fashioned and English roses – 700 varieties. Free catalogue. www.davidaustinroses.com Tel: 01902 376300

Tough and spacious garden bag, perfect for collecting leaves, branches and grass. Strong enough even for those prickly rose cuttings! Folds flat for compact storage. Capacity 245 litres. £5.00. Many other useful products available. Call 0845 658 5588 or access our website: www.evengreener.com

C You are going to read some short descriptions of TV programmes. Look at these questions (1–11) and then scan the descriptions to find the answers. Write the letters A – J in the spaces. You will need to use one letter more than once.

**Which programme**

| | | |
|---|---|---|
| would you watch if you were interested in football? | 1 | _____ |
| is about painting or sculpture? | 2 | _____ |
| may be helpful if you are thinking of moving house? | 3 | _____ |
| will give an insight into travelling to remote places? | 4 | _____ |
| is about famous people's reactions to a situation? | 5 | _____ |
| will tell you if it's going to rain tomorrow? | 6 | _____ |
| offers a couple of hours of pure relaxation and escapism? | 7 | _____ |
| is likely to provide some useful tips for a weekend away? | 8 | _____ |
| gives coverage of the latest events around the world? | 9 | _____ |
| may offer advice on how to keep fit and well? | 10 | _____ |
| may reveal something about the car you drive? | 11 | _____ |

A *News at Ten* with Alistair Sims    ITV1
*Weather*, Jane Fletcher

B *The King & the Pirate*    Movie Channel
Drama set in Scotland 100 years ago. Starring Mel Gibson.

C *The Big Match Replay*    Liverpool v Arsenal    Sky Sports 1

D *The Holiday Programme*    BBC1
Sarah Lloyd investigates self-catering in Wales and camping on Dartmoor.

E *For Art's Sake*    Channel 4
The new exhibitions at the Prado and the Louvre.

F *Health Check*    BBC2
Looking at the nation's health, with Andrew McKenna.

G *I'm a Celebrity ... Get Me Out of Here!*    ITV1
Ant & Dec host the first of the new series.

H *Location Location Location*    Channel 4
Kirsty & Phil help three young couples find their dream home.

I *Police, Camera, Action!*    ITV4
Jeff Acorah looks at vehicles which are unsuitable for the road.

J *Himalaya*, with Michael Palin    UKTV History
The intrepid reporter moves on to Tibet.

D You are going to read some short texts advertising different products. Read these questions and then choose from the products (A – H). Write the letters in the spaces.

**What would you buy**

| | | |
|---|---|---|
| for displaying a collection of china? | **1** | _____ |
| for preparing vegetables? | **2** | _____ |
| for squeezing oranges? | **3** | _____ |
| for making bread? | **4** | _____ |

**What would you use**

| | | |
|---|---|---|
| to clean and protect a motorbike? | **5** | _____ |
| to find out more about a pet? | **6** | _____ |
| when weeding a flowerbed? | **7** | _____ |

**A** Give your arms a rest with this mains-powered potato peeler, which can peel a kilo of potatoes in 2–4 mins. Easy-to-clean stainless steel blades and a safety switch. £49.95

**B** This comfortable portable beach chair can be put together in under 60 seconds. The tough canvas material ensures it will last for years. Only £24.95

**C** Liquid polish used by professionals to achieve that showroom shine on cars, bikes, boats and caravans. *Caress* protects against bad weather conditions. Apply at least twice a year. £10.99

**D** If you're mad about cats, then this is the book for you. *The Cat Manual* includes sections on cat nutrition and cat psychology. £8.95, including post & packing

**E** Your hands need protecting when doing those dirty jobs around the garden. Strong canvas gloves with double seams, in 3 sizes. £7.50 a pair

**F** Beautiful mahogany-look collector's rack – a series of shelves to show a cherished collection of ornaments to perfection. In kit form for you to assemble. £16.95

**G** Even if you've never baked a loaf before, nothing could be easier than adding the basic ingredients to this automatic bread maker and switching on. It does the rest! The deluxe model allows you to add extras like fruit and nuts. £85/£120

**H** Squeeze citrus fruit effortlessly with this mini juice extractor. Uses 4 AA batteries (not supplied). £19.95

# Practice 1

In these tasks you need to skim  for gist and scan  for information (see Units 1 and 2).

 **A** Read the questions first, then look quickly at the text to find the answers. Write short answers, in your own words.

1 Which country is the text about?

2 What did George III suffer from?

3 What dates are mentioned, and what happened on those dates?

4 Which four people are named, and what were their relationships with each other?

5 Where was George IV crowned king?

6 What was his reaction to becoming king?

7 Why had he married Princess Caroline?

8 Why did their marriage fail?

9 What was their daughter's name?

10 Why did Princess Caroline return to England?

11 What was she accused of?

12 What excuse was used to prevent Caroline becoming queen?

## KEEN TO BE KING

When George IV finally inherited the British throne, he had been waiting a long time for the opportunity to wield power and control his own finances. His father, George III, had suffered
5 from repeated bouts of mental illness (now thought to be caused by a hereditary blood disorder which modern-day drugs could have cured); contemporary treatment for this was so painful that it helped to turn his nervous breakdowns into
10 fits of insanity.

Even while George III was still alive, his son had been declared Prince Regent, in order to rule the country while the King recovered from his madness. But in 1820 George III finally died, and George IV
15 was crowned king in Westminster Abbey, to his great delight.

George IV's wife, Princess Caroline of Brunswick, was not crowned with him, or even allowed to attend the coronation. He had married her in
20 1795, hoping that Parliament would then pay off his debts and give him a much larger allowance. The marriage was disastrous, however, as the Prince took an instant dislike to her, and he did not even receive as much as he had hoped from Parliament. Even when Caroline produced an heir
25 to the throne, Princess Charlotte, the Prince did not relent. He sent Caroline to live in a modest house in Blackheath, south-east London, and only allowed her to visit her daughter once a fortnight. She soon tired of these restrictions, and spent
30 several years travelling around Europe, leading a colourful, adventurous life.

➔

When she heard of the old King's death, Caroline returned immediately to England, to be crowned queen with her husband. Popular opinion supported her, but her husband was insistent that she would never be queen. His attempts to prove that she had been guilty of immoral behaviour succeeded, but he still could not get the divorce he wanted. So Caroline was turned away from the door of Westminster Abbey, with the excuse that she had no ticket for the coronation, and George IV was crowned alone.

 **B** Read the questions first, then look quickly at the text to find the answers. Write short answers.

1 Why is it best to avoid this insect?

2 What is the insect's common name?

3 How many hairs does it have on its body?

4 What does its nest look like?

5 Where does the insect usually make its nest?

6 Which animals are particularly at risk from the insect?

7 What could happen to an animal affected by contact with the insect?

8 What should you do if your pet touches one of these insects?

9 In a public park, who should be responsible for eliminating these insects?

## INSECT TO BEWARE OF

Its Latin name is *Thaumetopoea processionea*, which sounds very impressive, but it is usually known as the processionary caterpillar. It's a small insect, only 3–5 cm long, and at one particular stage of its development its body is covered with an amazing number of microscopic hairs – about 600,000 of them! Unfortunately for us, each hair contains a chemical which many humans and animals are allergic to. In the Mediterranean area, it makes its nest at the top of pine trees, and if you look up, it's easy to see the big fluffy white ball which this caterpillar calls home. In the nest, the caterpillar goes through four stages of change, eventually turning into a moth.

These insects get their name from the way they walk in a line, one behind the other, and sadly this is a fascinating sight for most animals. Cats and dogs, in particular, are attracted to them, and may sniff the little furry insects or, worse still, try to lick them. Animals' tongues and throats can become severely inflamed because of this, and need immediate veterinary treatment, if serious injury or even death is to be averted. So make sure you never walk your dog in a pine forest in southern France, Italy, Spain or Greece, unless it's on a lead. Try to keep cats away from these areas. Call a vet at once if your pet has touched one of these caterpillars. Don't touch your pet yourself, or you too may experience skin problems.

On private land it's the owner's responsibility to get rid of these harmful insects, and on public land it's the job of the local authorities. It's not only the Mediterranean countries that suffer from this problem. Millions of these caterpillars have invaded Northern Europe too, and caused damage to thousands of trees.

C  You are going to read part of a leaflet produced by the local tourist information office for visitors to Winchester, in the south of England. Read the questions first, then look quickly at the text to find the answers. Write short answers.

1  What is the cathedral most famous for?
2  Is there an entrance fee?
3  Where in Winchester is the cathedral?
4  When was the earliest part of the cathedral built?
5  Which famous person is buried there?
6  How do you know who the guides are?
7  Which times are unsuitable for visiting the inside of the building?
8  How old are the sculptures in one of the chapels?

## WINCHESTER CATHEDRAL

The cathedral is situated between the railway station and the River Itchen. It is surrounded by attractive gardens, green spaces, and the narrow lanes and half-timbered buildings of this ancient city. It is well signposted, so finding it presents no problems for the visitor. It was built between the eleventh and thirteenth centuries and has stood the test of time well, although the tower was rebuilt in the twelfth century, and work is continually in progress to maintain the fabric of the building and prevent further decay.

Although it is best known for its large round painted table, supposed until very recently to be the original Round Table of the legendary King Arthur, a steady stream of visitors come to the cathedral to look at the grave of a writer. Jane Austen, the author of

25 *Pride and Prejudice* and other highly regarded novels, died in 1817 and was buried here.

It costs nothing to visit the cathedral, as free access has
30 always been granted to visitors, but we rely on your generosity to help us meet the costs of running the building – currently over £600,000 a year. Please make a donation if you
35 can.

You can wander round at your own pace, or you can ask the voluntary guides for help and information. They are easily
40 identified by their red badges. Please note the times of services in the cathedral – 8.00 am and 5.30 pm every day – and avoid these times for sightseeing if possible.

Don't miss the 12th-century wall 45 paintings and marble font, the 15th-century Great Screen, and the 20th-century sculptures in the Lady Chapel. These are all regarded as important artistic achievements in 50 their own right.

Educational visits are a feature of the cathedral's contribution to the community. However, if you wish to bring a school group, 55 please contact the information desk for details, as advance warning is needed.

# Intensive reading

 **Intensive reading** involves a very careful, thorough reading of a text. Underline or highlight words you do not know, and look them up or work out their meaning from context. Try to paraphrase difficult words or groups of words. When you come to the end, read the text again, several times if necessary, until you feel you really understand all of it.

A  Read this text carefully and answer the questions which follow.

## A GREENER BRAZIL

Although Brazil has its share of environmental and social problems, it has its successes too. One of these is the town of Curitiba, where the authorities
5  have shown evidence of a strong vision and commitment to good environmental practice. In the shanty towns there are no flies or litter, because there is a voluntary recycling exchange system. A constant
10  procession of women and children bring rubbish they have collected in bags or on wheelbarrows; for a kilo of litter they are given a kilo of potatoes and one of bananas. So the streets stay clean, and
15  people don't go hungry.

Public transport has also been transformed. The buses are of the latest design with platforms that open out at the same time as the doors, enabling a large
20  number of passengers to board quickly.

People buy their tickets beforehand to save time, and buses travel in their own dedicated bus lanes. These recent initiatives have reduced traffic delays in the rush hour and have encouraged far  25 more Curitiba residents on to public transport. Many motorists now leave their cars at home and take the bus to work.

Jaime Lerner, former mayor of Curitiba,  30 is proud of what he and his colleagues have achieved. He says, 'I'm convinced that every city in the world, whatever the scale, whatever the financial resources, can bring about a significant change in  35 less than two years. What is needed is the will to change, and the involvement of all its citizens. That's what we had in Curitiba.'

**1** Which words in the first paragraph mean the following?
  **a**  area of poor housing
  **b**  rubbish or waste
  **c**  unpaid, not compulsory
**2** Who keeps parts of Curitiba clean and tidy, and why?
**3** What is the main advantage of the new type of bus?
**4** Which other improvements to bus travel have reduced traffic delays in Curitiba?
**5** According to Jaime Lerner, which two things are essential when trying to solve the problems of city life?
**6** How has life improved in recent years for Curitiba residents? Write a paragraph of about 30 words.

B  Read this text carefully and answer the questions which follow.

## UP, UP AND AWAY

People are always asking me what the difference is between charter flights and scheduled flights. Well, it's simple really – most business and long-haul flights are operated by international airlines, which offer a scheduled timetable of flights to choose from. The more recently established budget (or low-cost) airlines also operate scheduled flights. Charter flights, on the other hand, are organised by the major tour operators, who use them to transport their package holiday customers to popular holiday resorts abroad, but who often offload their spare seats to the general public via travel agents or websites.

Finding cheap flights is a complicated business that even seasoned travel agents find a challenge. The best thing to do, if you have time, is to shop around; while most companies offer cheap flights, none can guarantee the best deals to all destinations. The cheapest flight may not be the cheapest option: a flight which returns at three in the morning may mean you have to get an expensive taxi home, and some airports are a long way from the city centre, so transport costs will be an issue.

Many travel websites and travel agents won't offer both scheduled and charter flights, and few will offer flights on low-cost airlines, as the latter offer no commission to agents and encourage customers to book direct with them for the cheapest fares. Charter flights are priced low because the planes are kept full; tickets are discounted heavily to sell seats right up to check-in time. So wait until shortly before you travel to get the best bargains. If, on the other hand, you're interested in getting a cheap scheduled flight, be flexible with your dates (midweek fares are usually cheaper), be prepared to fly indirect or leave at an unsocial hour, and book well in advance.

1  What does the writer tell us about scheduled flights in the first paragraph?
   A  They are safer than charter flights.
   B  They are only organised by long-established airlines.
   C  They are advertised by travel agents and websites.
   D  They offer the customer more choice.

2  In the second paragraph, the writer advises people who want cheap tickets to
   A  accept a good travel agent's recommendations.
   B  research offers from many different companies.
   C  buy tickets quickly in order to get a bargain.
   D  go for the cheapest tickets they can find.

3  What is the best way of getting a cheap charter flight, according to the text?
   A  Book at the last minute.
   B  Offer a choice of dates.
   C  Be ready to fly during the night.
   D  Consider flying to another airport first.

C  Read this text carefully and answer the questions which follow.

# VOLUNTEERS FOR A LEISURE AMERICA

*Consumerism? Who needs it?* **Walter Schwarz** *on a growing trend of people opting for cheerful austerity.*

Lynn Kidder had two jobs – computer programming and teaching the piano. She and her husband earned several thousand dollars a month, but they
5  were too busy to be happy. Lynn wanted to play her piano, not teach it. So they took a course in Voluntary Simplicity (VS). They learned how to cut their spending and enhance their savings. After four years of Voluntary Simplicity, they achieved Crossover Point: they gave up all their jobs and joined the new leisured class.

10  Another couple reached the height of luxurious living in their late thirties. They had a new Audi, a new Jeep Cherokee and a boat on the lake, and went skiing abroad every year; but they 'felt insecure and unfulfilled'. So they signed up for the same course that Lynn went on – with the New Road Map Foundation, which teaches VS and FI (financial independence) in nine
15  punishing steps. Now they, too, have left their jobs, live in a small house on the interest from their investments – less than a third of the income they had before – and do only voluntary work.

Arnie Anfinson is a lithe and agile 78-year-old who spends much of his time on the internet and email, networking voluntary simplicity. He was a
20  meteorologist with United Airlines until he sold his house to his daughter and rented back the ground floor. Then he began to live cheerfully on less than $300 a month. Outside the back door he breeds worms for his garden, feeding them with kitchen waste. His clothes are secondhand. 'My emphasis is not on saving money but on spending responsibly for the environment.
25  I eat to live.'

The newly leisured call themselves downshifters or downsizers. Nobody knows how many they are, or whether insecurity, stress or environmental concern is their main motive. But, according to Lynn Kidder, the rapidly spreading movement is 'recognised as a smarter way to live. You make space
30  in your life for what you really care about. How you do it is up to you.'

The downshifters' guru is Joe Dominguez, who died in 1997. In a big, comfortable, simple house in suburban Seattle, he set up the New Road Map Foundation. More than 3,000 people had taken his course on 'Transforming Your Relationship with Money and Achieving Financial Independence'
35  before he and his star ex-pupil Vicki Robin published *Your Money Or Your Life*. Dominguez was a Wall Street stock analyst until he retired at 30 to teach others to follow him. 'It struck a chord in all sorts of people – from yuppies to people on welfare – who felt they weren't managing money or getting value for things. After all, these are old American values: good
40  use of money, good bargains, and lack of show.' He found that mothers were the first to see that $10 earned wasn't worth an hour less with their children. 'Even little kids learned that an hour more with Mom was worth giving up $10-worth of gadgets.'

→

45 Downsizers aim to live with balance in order to find a life of greater purpose, fulfilment and satisfaction. Charlene MacMahon wrote in Seattle's 'Simple Living' newsletter: 'When you simplify your life, you do fewer (or none) of the things you don't like to do and more of the things you enjoy. And you seek out only those people and relationships which enhance your life. This is not about deprivation – this is about choices.'

1 What are the main aims of Voluntary Simplicity?

2 What happens at Crossover Point?

3 Why do you think the couple in the second paragraph felt 'insecure and unfulfilled'?

4 Which expression in the second paragraph means 'enrolled on' or 'registered for'?

5 What are Arnie Anfinson's current living arrangements?

6 What general point about modern society is Arnie making when he says 'I eat to live'?

7 Which organisation was set up by Joe Dominguez?

8 Who wrote *Your Money Or Your Life*?

9 Which expression in the paragraph beginning on line 31 means 'produced a response'?

10 According to the text, what are 'old American values'?

11 According to Charlene MacMahon, what do downshifters do more of?

12 What is downshifting or downsizing? Write a paragraph of about 50 words.

# Reading between the lines

 Sometimes you not only need to answer questions based on your understanding of the gist and the details of a text, but also to deduce meaning from the context. The answer you want may not be stated in black and white, but will be implicit in the text. Finding this is known as **reading between the lines**.

As you read a text, ask yourself, 'How does the writer or narrator feel? What is the atmosphere like? What would I do in this situation?' These are the kinds of questions which need a careful reading of the text and an understanding of its cultural, social and emotional background.

**A** Read these paragraphs and answer the questions.

> At first glance the village looked just the same, but then Joe realised the pond had been grassed over, and there was a car park where the cricket ground had been. He stood looking at the rows of shiny new cars on the asphalt where runs had been scored and matches won and lost. It seemed a waste, somehow.

**1** Has Joe been to the village before?

**2** Does he prefer it in the past or the present?

> Moira's room was on the second floor. There was no heating, and the wind blew under the door and down the chimney in wild, violent gusts. Moira shivered. Would tonight be one of the nights? Would the long-dead Baron make one of his regular appearances? Would he come to claim her as victim number three? She held her breath and listened. There was a scratching kind of noise outside her door.

**3** What do you think has happened in the story so far?

**4** Why do you think Moira shivers?

> Carole sighed as she put the letter back in the envelope. She knew they would have to go, although John probably wouldn't be keen. He was very busy these days with his new responsibilities, and looked so tired most of the time. What a pity Luxembourg was so far away, a long way to drive on your own, and anyway her boss certainly wouldn't let her take the time off at the moment. Perhaps later, when the summer rush was over ... She looked at the silver-framed photo on the piano, and smiled reassuringly at the white-haired old lady who was staring out at her. 'It's all right,' she whispered. 'I'll arrange it somehow. We'll be there.'

**5** Where is Carole planning to go, and who is she going to visit?

**6** What can you find out about the relationship between John and Carole?

**7** Which adjectives from the box best describe

    **a** Carole?     **b** John?     **c** neither of them?

| worried     hard-working     enthusiastic |
| --- |
| careful     caring     exhausted |

**B** Read this text carefully and answer the questions which follow.

Liz went into the library, hoping to find Mark. There was something important she wanted to say to him. He was sitting in his usual place, at one of the computers. He didn't look up when she spoke to him.

'Mark ... I ... How are you? Things OK?' She desperately wanted to keep the
5  tone light.

'Liz, hi. Yeah, I guess so. Just gotta get this essay typed out. The Prof's been hassling me for it for two weeks now.'

She sat down in the empty seat next to him and put her hand on his arm. 'Look, Mark, I need to talk to you. We ... need to talk. Don't we? Don't you agree?
10  Mark, please!' She was beginning to sound upset.

'Gimme a break, Liz. I gotta lot on my plate just now.' His fingers were still playing over the computer keyboard and his eyes stared fixedly at the screen.

She took a few deep breaths. Keep calm, she told herself. He always hated it if she started crying. 'OK, Mark,' she said. 'Shall we go for a coffee after the
15  seminar? It's Tuesday, remember. We could go to that Italian place.'

'No chance, babe,' he said. 'I'm cutting the seminar – need time to finish this.'

Liz stood up. 'Well, see you around, then.'

'Yeah, catch you later.'

**1** What kind of relationship do you think Liz and Mark have?

**2** What do you think she wants to talk to him about?

**3** Who do you think is more interested in their relationship, Liz or Mark? Why?

**4** From the text, what can you tell about

    **a** Liz's character?     **b** Mark's character?     **c** Mark's nationality?

**5** What do you think Liz means when she says, 'It's Tuesday, remember'?

**6** What does 'catch you later' mean? (Guess if you don't know.)

**7** What do you think happens next in the story?

**8** Do you sympathise more with Liz, or Mark? Why?

**9** Which adjectives from the box would you choose to describe Liz's and Mark's characters or attitudes? Justify your choices.

| sympathetic    helpful    selfish    moody    sensitive |
| --- |
| emotional    disciplined    passionate    tactful    patient |
| hard-working    uninterested    flexible    rude |

C  Read this text carefully and answer the questions which follow.

Jade waited until the man had gone into the café, and then, after glancing up and down the street to make sure no one was keeping an eye on her, she went inside after him. Her instructions were not to let him out of her sight, and she'd spent the whole day following him all
5  over town. She wasn't tired, far from it – but she hadn't eaten for hours and couldn't help thinking that a cup of coffee would go down well just now.

She selected a table right behind him to sit at, and congratulated herself on her choice when, almost immediately, he pressed a
10  couple of keys on his phone and started speaking to someone. She could hear every word he said, and unobtrusively took out her notebook to jot down what she could.

'OK, what's the news, Tiff? ... The next consignment's arriving Friday? Yeah, well, that's good ... No, the boys and me'll be ready ... Usual
15  place, then ... No problem about the cash? ... Well, as long as you're sure ...'

As she scribbled furiously in her notebook, she wondered how on earth he had got himself involved in all this. He had nice hair, she thought. His sunglasses were pushed up above his forehead,
20  and he was wearing a well-cut jacket with jeans. He seemed like the kind of man who, under different circumstances, she might ... She sighed, and told herself firmly not to be silly. This was a job, after all, and the probability was that he would end up in prison.

25  Her pen ran out, and as she turned away from him to delve in her bag for another, he swivelled silently round in his chair and gave her a long, critical look. By the time she turned towards him again, he was back in his original position, finishing his conversation and making another call, as if he were completely unaware of her presence. For
30  a moment she relaxed back in her seat, letting her mind run over the events of the day while she sipped her latte. She didn't notice two large strangers in dark suits enter the café, until they approached her table and one of them put a beefy hand on her arm.

1  What do you think Jade's job is?
2  What do you think she is trying to find out?
3  How do you think she feels about the man?
4  Do you think she knows that he has noticed her? Why or why not?
5  From the text, what can you tell about
   a  Jade's character?   b  the man's lifestyle?
6  What do you think 'unobtrusively' means (line 11)? Use the context to help you.
7  Why do you think the two strangers have come up to Jade?
8  What do you think happens next in the story?

D  Read this text carefully and answer the questions which follow.

**My life on:** Thursday 10 October
**Weight:** 10 stone 6 lb (too fat)
**Chocolate:** 3 Mars bars (too many)

Can't believe that Mariska didn't wake me up. What's the point of
5  sharing with her – waking people up is the only thing she's good at!
So no chance of getting to work on time. Arrived to a chorus of 'Late
again!' from my so-called friends and colleagues. You'd think they might
want to co-operate a bit and keep quiet about it, but no. So naturally
Deepak hears the noise and comes out of his executive office (probably
10  had to interrupt all sorts of important work to do so), and really ticks me
off. Silence falls while he tells me, 'I've had enough, do you understand?
This is a workplace, not a social club you pop into occasionally!' and
'You'll have to do better in future! Let me down one more time and
you're out of here!' Meanwhile I'm in a bit of a daze, still half asleep, to
15  tell the truth. It's not that I don't get on with Deepak – he's a really good
boss and makes lots of good decisions. But this is all a bit over the top.
I mean, how often have I been late this week? About ten minutes on
Monday (bus was late), half an hour on Tuesday (couldn't decide what
to wear), hardly at all yesterday – so what's he going on about?
20  Anyway, finally got away and went to my desk. Worked solidly for at
least an hour (am a serious, responsible worker, highly valued by the
company), then, when Deepak went off to a meeting, sneaked out for
a breath of fresh air in the park. Lovely bright sunshine, young couples
hand in hand, ah me! Love is in the air! Unfortunately sat on a bench
25  where someone had left their chips and tomato ketchup, and ruined
my new cream trousers. Rushed back to the Ladies at work and made
the stain a whole lot worse by scrubbing it. Had to keep my coat on
for the rest of the day to cover it up. Got awfully hot, as office central
heating is now on.
30  Evening passed quietly, with a light supper of microwaved pasta in some
sort of unidentifiable sauce, and absolutely zero to watch on TV. Gave
Mariska a stern warning: 'You'll have to do better in future! Let me down
one more time and you're out of here!' and went off to bed.

1  Who does the narrator blame for making her late for work, and why?
2  How does she feel about her office colleagues, and why?
3  How does she feel about her boss, Deepak?
4  How would you describe her attitude to work?
5  What does 'sneaked out' mean (line 22)? Use the context to help you.
6  Do you think she enjoyed her evening? How do you know?
7  What is her solution to the problem of her lateness?
8  What do you think her main interests in life are? Which phrases give you
the answer?

# Practice 2

In these tasks you need to read intensively 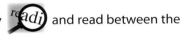 and read between the lines (see Units 3 and 4).

 **A** Read this text carefully and answer the questions which follow. Only one answer (A, B, C or D) is correct.

## THIEVES CUT OFF IN THEIR CRIME
### By Ray Massey – Motoring Correspondent

An inventor working in his garden shed has developed a device which enables police to track and then stop stolen cars by remote control. A satellite signal to an electronic gadget hidden in the vehicle locks the doors as it is automatically slowed down, leaving the baffled thief helpless inside. The prototype for the cigarette-pack-sized immobilising device was tested on an old Volvo. Now its inventor and the police hope it will be approved for use on public roads, and this will enable a manufacturer to go into full production.

The system, provisionally called KeepSafe, will make it possible for car owners who discover their vehicle has been stolen to retrieve it – and probably trap the thief – with one phone call. They will be answered by a recorded voice asking them to key in a special code number, using the phone's keypad. This gives access to the system. They will then connect to the police national computer by pressing a set of numbers which automatically register the car as stolen. An officer, seeing the message flash up on a screen, will start the next stage of the process. The gadget will be activated by a signal from the police. This will initially enable the car to be traced and tracked by satellite. Once the police are satisfied there is no danger to other drivers, a coded call to the engine immobiliser will slow down the car in stages of 10 or 20 mph until it comes to a halt – with doors and windows locked. Police patrol officers, alerted to the stolen car's progress, will be waiting to arrest the thief.

Inventor Niall Webster, 39, said: 'As a member of the public, I was fed up with all these people attempting to steal cars. I thought, surely we can do something to increase the recovery rates. The beauty of being a small-scale inventor is that I can lock myself in the garden shed to come up with ideas. This is the classic garden shed invention.'

Security consultant Colin Goodwin, who helped Mr Webster develop the system, said: 'As security devices become ever more sophisticated, car thieves are becoming increasingly resourceful. Existing alarms and immobilisers mean the thieves cannot start the car. So instead, they are resorting to hijackings

→

or breaking into homes to steal the keys. The joy of our system is that, even if they succeed in getting the keys, they can still 60 be stopped. The thief or joyrider doesn't know the police are chasing, and will be at a loss when the power starts to gradually fade from the engine.'

The inventor believes that, at a cost of under £500, the device will prove 65 popular with car owners. He has set up a company in Grimsby to develop it further, and is negotiating with a number of manufacturers.

**1** Where should the anti-crime device be fitted?

   **A** in a cigarette packet

   **B** in a shed

   **C** in a satellite

   **D** in a car

**2** What does 'baffled' mean in line 7?

   **A** frightened

   **B** puzzled

   **C** shocked

   **D** trapped

**3** What does 'it' refer to in line 18?

   **A** the device

   **B** the car

   **C** the phone call

   **D** the recorded voice

**4** Before deciding to stop the stolen car, the police will check that

   **A** the device is functioning.

   **B** the thief is still in the car.

   **C** no motorists are nearby.

   **D** no roads are blocked.

**5** Which feature of his work does Niall Webster say he appreciates?

   **A** the limited scope of his inventions

   **B** the comfort of his workplace

   **C** the opportunity to talk to the public

   **D** the old-fashioned approach he has developed

**6** According to Colin Goodwin, one advantage of the device is that

   **A** it will be sold at a reasonable price.

   **B** cars will no longer need alarms.

   **C** no new ways of stealing cars will be found.

   **D** thieves will be unaware that they have been detected.

B Read this text carefully and answer the questions which follow. Only one answer (A, B, C or D) is correct.

## WAITING GAME IS STRICTLY FOR PROS

*Some people are mean when it comes to tipping, writes* **Jane Headon**.

In the United States, waiting at tables is more a profession than a job. Wages are token and staff expect to live off their tips. The more professional the service given, the more substantial the reward. During a bout of postgraduate travel, I waited at tables in New York, including one Wall Street restaurant; I was disappointed if my tips didn't exceed $400 a week. In Britain, the experience tells a different tale. Money and respect are handed out in more carefully guarded measures to those who serve food.

Yet lack of respect hasn't stopped students from taking waiting jobs to eke out a steadily shrinking bank balance. Nicola Sizer is 28 and finishing a four-year teaching degree at Goldsmiths College. A large debt at the end of her first year forced her into waitressing at the Village Taverna, a Greek restaurant in south-east London. Most of her money comes from tips, but they're variable. 'Some nights, people don't leave you anything,' she says. 'People forget that the waitress isn't there to have a good time.'

Chris Pye waited at tables at five London restaurants over a three-year period. He worked for a time at Pasta Mania where, as in many restaurants, the official policy was that waiters had to pay for 'runners' (customers who leave without paying). 'I'd been waiting on a really nice couple for about an hour and had been having a good time with them,' he recalls. 'I turned my back for a couple of minutes and, when I turned round, they'd gone.' Outraged, Pye followed them across Soho, where he was rewarded by a punch in the face. 'It amazed me that two such apparently respectable people could abuse me in a way that they would never abuse their local shopkeeper.'

Dave Turnbull, district officer for the hotel and catering section of the Transport and General Workers' Union, admits there are particular problems with tipping. 'It depends on what form the tips are in,' he says. 'Also, there's nothing in law to say that the service charge goes to the waiter.' But he concedes that working at the right place can be financially very rewarding.

Jane Stocks is 34 and has been waitressing for five years. She's been at the Chicago Pizza Pie Factory in central London for one year. Waitressing is her career choice – she enjoys the social aspect of the work and the fact that her opinion counts. Outside, she doesn't always get treated so well. 'If I'm going to look for an apartment and I say that I'm a waitress, people say "Oh". When I'm applying for a credit card or a bank account, waitressing isn't the kind of job that they respect.'

Not everybody can handle waitressing. Gina Clough, aged 26, manages the Chicago Pizza Pie Factory where Jane works, and says countless waitresses have left in tears. 'People know a lot more about food these days,' she says. 'Going out for a meal used to be a treat. Nowadays anybody can eat out. It's a hard job waitressing. At the end of the day, if the customer's not happy, you're the one to blame.' Although she can point to waitresses earning tips of £150 on a good night, she is firmly of the opinion that it's not a job anybody can do. Jane Stocks agrees: 'You've got to be able to take a lot of responsibility, a lot of stress and concentrate on a lot of things for a long time. You've also got to be all different things to all people.'

1 The writer says that waiters in the USA
   A  receive low wages.
   B  are not given enough respect.
   C  find it easy to make money.
   D  find their work disappointing.

2 Nicola Sizer started waitressing because she wanted to
   A  enjoy herself.
   B  pay back some money.
   C  try a different profession.
   D  work in a Greek environment.

3 How did Chris Pye feel when his customers left the restaurant?
   A  irritated
   B  nervous
   C  angry
   D  upset

4 Which problem does Dave Turnbull mention?
   A  Waiters are generally poorly paid.
   B  Many waiters don't join his union.
   C  Some waiters earn much more money than others.
   D  Waiters may not receive money intended for them.

5 Jane Stocks complains of the way she is treated
   A  by customers.
   B  by her boss.
   C  by financial companies.
   D  by selfish colleagues.

6 What does 'a treat' mean in lines 74 – 5?
   A  a family event
   B  a light snack
   C  a formal ceremony
   D  a special occasion

7 Gina Clough thinks that waiting at tables is hard because
   A  customers expect a lot.
   B  evening work is tiring.
   C  the standard of cooking has gone up.
   D  the staff blame each other for mistakes.

# Speed reading

 If you have a long text to skim or scan, you may need to read it fast in order to answer questions in the allotted time. Here are some ways of improving **the speed of your reading**:

- Do not read each word. You have not got time for this.
- Look at each paragraph, and let your eye travel quickly over it, picking out important words like nouns, verbs, names, dates, etc.
- Split the text into **groups of words**, and let your eye travel from one group to another, helped by the linking words.
- Read as much as you can (newspapers, magazines, short stories), just for the gist, without paying attention to style, grammar or vocabulary.
- **Time yourself** when reading. How long do you take to read a paragraph, or a page of closely typed print? Aim to reduce the time it takes you to read a particular text.

A Look quickly at this text **for one minute only**. Then cover up the text and write down every word you can remember. You should remember at least some of the words in bold, which will give you the gist of the passage.

> Despite the **traffic** which can be extremely heavy at times, **Athens** is a most **attractive capital city**, as **tourists** have **discovered** over the years. One of the most **appealing areas** is **Plaka**, where **picturesque tavernas** rub shoulders with **souvenir shops** in a patchwork quilt of **nineteenth-century buildings, lanes and squares**. Several **fascinating museums** are housed in **beautifully restored mansions** ...

B Now look at the following text. Which do you think are the most important words for understanding the meaning? Underline, circle or highlight them. You can take your time over this.

> Are you a chocoholic? If so, you would probably have felt at home in the ancient Mayan civilisation of Central America. In this sophisticated culture – noted for its outstanding achievements in architecture, astronomy, chronology, painting and pottery – chocolate played a central role, appreciated as a drink and used as form of currency. Chocolate, which comes from the cacao bean, has been around for at least three thousand years, and has been consumed as a drink for most of that time.

C First read these questions. Then read the text which follows **for three minutes only**. Answer the questions using short answers.

1 Which country do the islands belong to?
2 What is the food like on Hayman Island?
3 Where did Captain Cook land in 1770?
4 Which is the southernmost island, according to the text?
5 Where would you go for a *quiet* holiday?
6 Which island would you visit for diving?
7 Where is the largest sandy beach in the world, according to the text?

# THE ISLANDS OF QUEENSLAND

Queensland is home to some of the most magical islands and the largest expanse of coral in the world. It may well be the closest you ever get to paradise. You can while away the hours on
5 a deserted palm-fringed beach, cruise around the coral reef, or throw yourself into the various watersports. Scattered like jewels in the Pacific Ocean, these Australian islands stretch from Lady Elliott in the south to Lizard in the north, and all
10 are a delight to visit.

Hayman Island, in the Whitsundays, is probably one of the most luxurious resorts in the world, with dreamy beaches, exotic wildlife and mouth-watering cuisine. For something a little more exclusive, try Bedarra, privately owned and with 15 only sixteen villas. For a touch of history, go to Lizard Island, where Captain Cook landed in 1770. This is also where divers go. To get away from it all, go to Heron Island, a haven of peace and quiet. Fraser Island has the largest sandy beach 20 in the world, Hook has a wonderful National Park ... the list is endless.

D First read this text **for three minutes only**. Then turn over and answer the questions which follow.

# GYPSIES IN BRITAIN

Gypsies, the Romany-speaking people scattered throughout Europe and North America who maintain their nomadic way of life in our industrialised society, migrated from north-west
5 India from the ninth century onwards. They were first recorded in Britain before 1500, and were originally known as 'Egyptians', as it was assumed they had come from Egypt. (The word *Gypsy* derives from *Egyptian*.)
10 Throughout the centuries there have been many attempts to expel and punish them, and to attack their culture and way of life. Only recently have local authorities been obliged to provide sites for Gypsies and other travellers to use as a temporary home. It is true to say that Gypsy 15 people have suffered severely over the years, but their nomadic lifestyle makes the provision of education and healthcare problematic. There are over 100,000 Gypsies in Britain today, many of whom do not have access to all the services that 20 might be expected of a civilised society.

1 Where did Gypsies come from originally, according to the text?

2 When did they first appear in Britain, as far as we know?

3 Where does the name 'Gypsy' come from?

4 What is their language called?

5 What are the two main services some Gypsies are not receiving?

6 How many Gypsies are there in Britain?

E First read this text **for five minutes only**. Then cover it up and answer the questions which follow.

# TV EXPOSURE DAMAGES CHILDREN'S SPEECH

## By Sarah Boseley

Too much television is stunting the language development of middle-class children as well as those from deprived inner-city areas, according to a leading speech therapist. Dr
5 Sally Ward, who is considered the country's leading authority on the speech development of young children, believes babies under one year old should not watch television at all. Children of two or three should watch for no
10 more than an hour an day.

Dr Ward's ten-year study of babies and toddlers in inner-city Manchester showed television was a very important factor in delaying the speech development of the one
15 in five children found to have problems. The background noise from televisions stopped them learning to talk as early as they should. At eight months, they neither recognised their names nor basic words like 'juice' and
20 'bricks'. At three, they had the language of two-year-olds.

Now she has found that children from well-to-do families at her London clinic are being handicapped in the same way. 'The television is being used as a babysitter, by 25 nannies particularly. Some of these middle-class children are spending far too much time watching television and DVDs. They get very fixed on the colours and flashing lights. They are riveted by the screen. We found in our 30 study that it was quite difficult to get them interested in toys.'

All the evidence, says Dr Ward, shows that children whose language is below standard at the age of three can be set back for life. 35 'They are likely to be educational failures in all sorts of ways. They will go to school with depressed language levels, and their whole educational progress is held back.' In her Manchester study, Dr Ward found that 40 parents who were taught to turn off the television and talk to their children could quickly repair the damage. Babies of nine months would be back on course within four months.

1 What is the speech therapist's name?

2 How much TV should children younger than one year old watch?

3 How much TV should two- and three-year-olds watch?

4 How long did the research project last?

5 Which city did it take place in?

**F** First read these questions. Then read the text which follows **for five minutes only**, and answer the questions.

**1** Which country did the first well-known Siamese twins come from?

**2** How long did they live?

**3** What do their names mean?

**4** How did they make a lot of money?

**5** When did they die?

## THE ORIGINAL SIAMESE TWINS

Twin babies joined together at some part of their bodies are known as Siamese or conjoined twins. Although the tendency these days is to operate on the twins, in order to separate them and allow them to lead independent lives, some have lived together for many years without being surgically separated. In fact, the original Siamese twins lived for sixty-three years joined together. They were born in 1811 in Siam, the country now known as Thailand, and were called Chang and Eng, meaning 'left' and 'right' in the Thai language. It is because Chang and Eng became so well known during their lifetime that twins born joined together were called Siamese twins. Nowadays, 'conjoined twins' is the preferred term.

Chang and Eng shared no organs, but were connected by an arm-like tube between their bodies, which did not appear to cause them any problems. As children, they swam in the Mekong river, catching fish for their mother, and were noticed by an English businessman, who realised what a fascinating sight Europeans would find them. He therefore took them to Europe, and thus the twins' career began.

At that time, circuses and travelling shows were extremely popular: people would happily pay to see anything unusual. And when a sea captain, Abel Coffin, took over the twins and took them to America, their nationwide tours were a sell-out. Chang and Eng, however, wanted to keep their dignity as far as possible, and once they reached legal adulthood at the age of twenty-one, they took charge of their own affairs, and only allowed themselves to be on show with a certain reluctance and numerous restrictions. People were not permitted to approach and touch them, for example. Their aim was to achieve respectability at all costs.

They were not anxious to undergo what was then a complex and dangerous operation to separate them, and seemed content to be joined. Once they had made a considerable sum, they settled in North Carolina in the USA and lived comfortably there for more than forty years. Unfortunately they were on the losing side in the American Civil War: when the South surrendered in 1865, they lost their comfortable position and income. So they were obliged to tour the country again, and were on show in other countries around the world.

Over the years, Chang's moods had become darker and he had started drinking. On their way back from Russia by sea, he fell ill with lung disease, which eventually killed him, and his brother too, in 1874.

# Topic, source and register

It is often helpful to be able to identify what a reading text is about (the **topic**), where it comes from (the **source**), and what style of writing it is (the **register**). Here are some ways of achieving this.

**Topic** – skim for gist, and then the topic will become clear.

**Source** – scan the text to find answers to these questions:

* Is there a heading or a title? If so, it may be a newspaper or magazine article.
* Is there an ending like 'Best wishes'? If so, it may be a letter or an email.
* Does it have short forms or incomplete sentences? If so, it may be a note or an email.

**Register** – scan the text to find the answers to these questions:

* Are there contractions or incomplete sentences? If so, the register is informal.
* Are there complex structures and high-level vocabulary? If so, it is formal.
* Is there any slang or colloquial language? If so, it is informal.

**A** Match each of these short extracts (1 – 7) with its probable source (A – H). There is one extra source.

1 Don't forget to wear fancy dress! And can you possibly come early?

2 All claims for expenses must be submitted to Accounts with receipts.

3 I'm dying to hear how it all goes, so don't keep me in suspense too long!
All the best, anyway.

4 Melt the sugar and butter together in a saucepan and slowly fold in first the dry ingredients and then the beaten eggs.

5 Anyone out there planning to drive to Keele University this weekend? Can share petrol costs. Contact Dave on 07812 945881

6 Unfortunately no time today to go the bank. Kept busy by MB – even worked through my lunch hour! Terribly hot all afternoon.

7 It is important to eat a variety of foods in order to maintain a balanced diet. There are so many different types of fruit and vegetables on sale nowadays that it has never been easier.

**A** recipe    **B** notice    **C** invitation    **D** instructions for staff
**E** letter    **F** diary    **G** novel    **H** leaflet on healthy eating

B Look at these sentences and decide what each one is about. For each sentence, choose the appropriate topic (A – K). There is one extra topic. Use each topic once only.

1 Police are hoping the public will come forward with information regarding the violent attack on two teenage boys over the weekend.

2 Some of the highest earning Hollywood stars have assembled in a San Francisco studio to record a single which will be sold in aid of the world's poor.

3 The recent wet weather has caused problems for local strawberry farmers, who say their harvest will be badly affected this year.

4 Any supporter found committing acts of vandalism will be banned from future matches, and may be prosecuted.

5 And so it's forty love to Isabelle Martinez, thanks to that really brilliant backhand of hers – it looks as if she's going to win the match! Don't you think so, John?

6 Boiling vegetables for a long time removes the vitamins they contain, and also reduces their taste.

7 He's going to trek overland through India, I think, with a whole group of people – he'll be away for months, of course. I bet he'll love it!

8 I don't suppose there's anything at all on – I haven't seen a good film for years, have you?

9 On Wall Street today the pound fell sharply against the dollar but regained its position by close of trading.

10 You need to slap lots of moisturiser on if you've been out in the sun – it takes a lot out of the skin and really dries it up. That's what I find, anyway.

A charity   B punishment   C agriculture   D sport   E money   F beauty
G travel   H food   I crime   J cinema   K radio

C Now look again at 1 – 7 in Exercise A and 1 – 10 in Exercise B, and decide whether they are written in formal or informal register. Write F for formal and I for informal for each extract or sentence.

D Read these short texts. What is their topic, source and register?

1 In the event of fire, leave the building by the nearest available exit. Do not attempt to extinguish the fire.

2 *Sarah –*
*Josie rang. Will ring back later.*
*Just off to my mum's. Remember to put the chicken on!*
*See you later.*
*Helen*

3 Your policy is due for renewal on the date shown, and we invite you to renew it for a further twelve months at the premium quoted.

4 Please read this booklet before attempting to operate your DVD player, which has been manufactured using the most advanced technology available and the most modern production and testing methods.

5 *Who's taken my sandwiches? Put them back or else!*
*Jack*

**E** Read the text, and identify its topic, source and register, giving reasons for your decisions.

## BREATHING CAN BE FATAL

During an average year, about 50 people die from carbon monoxide poisoning in the UK, caused directly by fumes from home heating appliances which are subsequently discovered to be defective. Several hundred people a year are made ill by inhaling the fumes, and have to have hospital treatment. These deaths and illnesses are unnecessary, and can easily be prevented.

Carbon monoxide has no colour, smell or taste, and it can kill. It can be given off by any equipment which burns a fossil fuel, such as coal, gas or oil. Fumes may build up in your home if the equipment is faulty, or if the chimney is blocked, or if the room does not allow circulation of fresh air. Watch out for any of the following: gas flames burning orange or yellow (they should be blue), dirty or sooty marks on or above a heater, and wood or coal stoves which burn slowly or go out. You yourself may feel sleepy, or have headaches, chest or stomach pains, sickness or sudden giddiness.

If you notice any of the above, stop using the appliance and call a qualified engineer. See your doctor at once if you have physical symptoms. Make sure your heaters are serviced regularly, have your chimneys swept once a year, and keep air vents and windows unblocked.

**F** Read the text, and identify its topic, source and register, giving reasons for your decisions.

## MOOLOOLABA RESIDENTS UPDATE

Hi there, friends and neighbours in the best beachside community in Australia! Thanks to all who attended the meeting with the police at the community hall last week. And for those who couldn't make it, here's what we talked about.

We heard a very helpful report from Herbie Minton, our Safer Community Co-ordinator. First, the good news – there has been NO reported crime in Parkyn Parade this year (seems incredible, but true, according to police records). In the Mooloolaba area as a whole, including Maroochydore and Alexandra Headland, a total of 832 crimes were reported this year; a number of these can be put down to the influx of visitors who find the Sunshine Coast so irresistible.

The bad news is that car theft is on the increase; this includes thefts of property from cars as well as the cars themselves, and accounts for almost a quarter of all the reported crimes. Our fabulous weather makes the situation worse, with car windows left open, and bags, cameras and so on left in view. So the message from Herbie and the police is: don't tempt the car thief! Don't leave anything valuable in your car, and if by chance you have to, hide it away so it isn't visible.

To read more online about what happened at the meeting, log on to www.mooloolabalife. com and click on **recent events**. Please do come and support us at the next meeting on 3rd November – it's your community, so make sure you have your say!

G  Do the same with the following text.

> Hi Peter
>
> Sorry I haven't replied before now, but it's manic at work, what with deadlines for a couple of big projects and software problems to deal with as well.
>
> 5  You asked about ways of reducing your fuel bills. Well, I think the experts agree that the most effective first step is to insulate your loft – you're losing a lot of heat through the roof if you don't. If you've already got a layer of traditional mineral or glass wool insulation, then leave it; it's not ideal, but getting rid of it is a hazardous process. But if your loft hasn't any insulation
>
> 10  at all, then we recommend you use one of the more natural alternatives, like wool, hemp, waste newspaper or waste cotton. They'll last for decades and won't harm the environment or your family. Whatever you use, there should be about 25 cm, or 10 inches, of insulation. Sounds thick, doesn't it? But you need it that thick to do the job.
>
> 15  If you want to know more about these 'greener' products, just let me know and I can send you some leaflets or give you a few website addresses, so you can do your own research.
>
> Hope all's well with the family. We may be seeing you over New Year, Rosie tells me.
>
> 20  All the best
>
> Graham

# Practice 3

In these tasks you need to speed read  and identify a text's topic, source and register  (see Units 5 and 6).

## REMEMBER:

- To speed read, let your eye travel quickly over each paragraph, picking out important words and phrases.
- To identify the source and topic, look for clues in the layout and vocabulary.
- To identify the register, check for contractions, slang and colloquial language.

 **A** Read each text **for one minute only**. Then answer the following questions.

**1** What is the topic of each text?

**2** What is the probable source of each text?

**3** Which register is used (formal/informal)?

> Most of us think it's a relatively simple task to buy bunches of fresh herbs from the local supermarket. But it's even easier to sow the seeds in pots and grow them on your kitchen windowsill. Then you can cut the herbs whenever you want, and just add a sprinkle to your soups and casseroles. They'll give your dishes that wow factor, and what's more, add vitamins to the family's diet. Get the meal on the table, sit back and enjoy the compliments!

 **B** Do the same with this text.

> I remember I first became interested in this kind of music when my parents took me to a concert in Vienna. I suppose I must have been about four – or maybe a bit older. I'll never forget the bright lights, and the elegantly dressed orchestra, and the excitement, and all those waves of wonderful sound washing over me. I got the bug, and since then I've learnt to play three instruments. I even enjoy practising scales!

 **C** Do the same with this text.

> This swimming pool is for the sole use of hotel guests and health club members and employees. Please note that this facility is not supervised or lifeguarded. Children or weak swimmers should be supervised at all times by those who are responsible for them. The hotel is not liable for any claims arising out of injury or the effects of injury, howsoever caused.

**D** Do the same with this text.

> I give the whole of my estate to be divided between my said children in equal shares absolutely, provided that if any of them shall have predeceased me, leaving children living at the date of my death, then such children shall on attaining the age of eighteen years receive in equal shares the share which their parent would otherwise have received.

**E** First read this text **for two minutes only**. Then cover it up and answer the questions which follow.

## MAGIC MARGARINE

We have known for a long time that diets rich in cholesterol are damaging to health. Throughout the developed countries of the world, people who are worried about their blood pressure
5 and the risk of heart disease have been cutting down on their intake of animal fats, and a low-cholesterol diet is prescribed for anyone in a high-risk category.

In 1995 a food product proven to reduce
10 cholesterol concentrations in the body was launched in Finland. Its name is Benecol, and it is a margarine spread containing what are known as plant stanols, derived from wood pulp. People who took part in a year-long study in Finland
15 consumed around three grams of stanols every day – equivalent to spreading three slices of toast with the margarine – and results of tests on the subjects of the study showed that their concentrations of total cholesterol were reduced
20 by up to ten per cent. Since that first study, a similar effect has been observed in other trials.

Scientists had been aware for some time that plant stanols, normally discarded as unwanted in the making of wood pulp, can lower blood cholesterol. Then Benecol's Finnish producers, a 25 food and chemicals company, discovered a way of making plant stanols soluble in vegetable oil. This means they can be consumed in the form of margarine, yogurt, cheese, ice cream or even chocolate – a range of products to appeal to 30 everyone's taste.

Regular consumption of Benecol does not necessarily guarantee reduced mortality from coronary heart disease, but it seems likely, taking other studies into account, that ten per cent 35 reduction in cholesterol would translate into a twenty per cent reduction in the risk of coronary heart disease. Since 1999 the product has been on sale in countries around the world, in the form of dairy products as well as margarine, and sales 40 are high.

**1** When was Benecol first sold to the public?

**2** In which country was it first developed?

**3** What is it made from?

**4** Why is it good for people's health?

**5** Which register is used in the text?

F  First read this text, an extract from a book called *The Seven Wonders of the Ancient World*, **for five minutes only**. Then cover it up and answer the questions which follow.

# THE GREAT PYRAMID AT GIZA

The only one of the Seven Wonders of the Ancient World that still exists is also the oldest of them all. The Great Pyramid at Giza in Egypt was built some time around 2560 BC; it was already two
5 thousand years old when work began on the next Wonder, the Hanging Gardens of Babylon. The age of the Great Pyramid – more than 4,500 years – is so great that it seems almost as if it has been there for ever, and that it will last for ever. In the words
10 of the Arab proverb, 'Man fears Time, but Time fears the Pyramids.'

But age is only one of the reasons why the Great Pyramid is so extraordinary. Another is its size: it is by far the largest of the Seven Wonders and,
15 except for frontier walls such as the Great Wall of China, it is the largest single thing made of stone that has ever been built. Then, too, there is the amazing effort and skill that were needed to cut all that stone and put it together into what is a near-
20 perfect geometrical form, with only simple tools and technology. In fact, if we were asked today for a list of Seven Wonders, ancient or modern, the

Great Pyramid would certainly still be on it. But why was such an extraordinary thing ever built? What exactly is it? 25

The Great Pyramid, like the other larger pyramids in Egypt, is the burial place, or tomb, of one of the country's ancient kings. During the period in Egyptian history know as the Old Kingdom (3100 – 2180 BC), more than twenty pyramids were built 30 at different places along the River Nile. Three of the larger ones are at Giza, which is now a suburb of Cairo. Like all the other pyramids, they are on the west bank of the Nile, with only the desert and the setting sun beyond. To the ancient Egyptians, the 35 west was the home of the dead. This was where the sun-god Ra, who sailed across the sky in his boat during the day, began his nightly journey down through the Underworld.

For a person's spirit to survive death, the 40 Egyptians believed the body had to be preserved. This was because the spirit of the dead person left the body at night, but had to return to it in the morning for food and rest. Without these things,

→

45 the soul would be lost. Members of a family, or their priests, would therefore place food in the tomb of a dead relative, together with furniture and the other necessities of life. So that the returning spirit would recognise its home, the body had to be kept 50 as lifelike as possible, which is why the Egyptians perfected the art of embalming bodies to produce what we now call mummies. We do not know what the ordinary people, who could not afford to pay for embalming, thought would happen to 55 their spirits after their bodies had decayed. Perhaps they simply accepted that, in death as in life, they would not be as lucky as their rulers.

Their king, or pharaoh, was considered to be a god – a son, in fact, of the sun-god Ra – and his body had to be especially well protected after 60 death. We can therefore understand why the pyramid which was his royal tomb was so large: by placing the mummy of the dead pharaoh deep inside such a huge structure, the builders thought that no one would ever be able to disturb it. 65 The shape of the structure was important too: a pyramid represented the rays of the sun as they spread out and touched the earth.

**1** What are the two most surprising facts about the Great Pyramid?

**2** What are the two questions which are asked and answered in the text?

**3** Why did the Ancient Egyptians embalm dead bodies?

**4** What did the Ancient Egyptians call their king?

**5** Which register is used in the text?

 **G** First read this text **for one minute only**. Then cover it up and answer the questions which follow.

Will you be overwhelmed by the sheer number of films to choose from this New Year? With so many being shown over the festive period, it's pretty near impossible to know what to watch, what to record and what to avoid. So that's why we've put together this great guide for you, 5 packed with hundreds of in-depth reviews and including 30 new entries from the past twelve months. You'll get outstanding coverage of world cinema, underground releases and experimental pictures, as well as cast, character, writing and directing credits.

To order your copy at the exclusive price of £19.99, including post and 10 packing, call 0870 770 7878 and have your credit card ready. Delivery within 28 days of receipt of order.

**1** What is the topic?

**2** What is the source?

**3** Which register is used?

# Multiple Choice

# Unit 7

A **multiple-choice** task offers you a series of statements or questions about the text, with three or four alternative answers to choose from. Questions may focus on factual details and features of text organisation, as well as gist, opinions, attitudes, etc.

Here are some tips for dealing with this:

- First read the text intensively (see Unit 3).
- Read between the lines to understand the writer's or character's feelings and situation (see Unit 4).
- Read the questions without looking at the options (A – C or A – D).
- Find the answers in the text.
- Choose the options which are closest to your own answers.
- Check that you are really answering the question.
- Watch out for distractors.

You are going to read a newspaper article about a competition. Choose the most appropriate answer (A, B, C or D) to each question.

## WRITING FOR REWARD

As much as $30,000 is waiting to be won in an International Short Story Competition, sponsored by the International Writers' Group (IWG), based in San Francisco. A total of 25 prizes will be awarded over the next twelve months. The closing date for entries is 31 December. The competition is open to all writers and entry is free.

'I'm delighted we're extending our sponsorship to Europe this year,' IWG President, Sam Payne, said yesterday. 'The judges are hoping for some really high-quality entries. Our past competitions in the USA have always been extremely successful, with some famous writers participating. Of course, what most writers are looking for is recognition of their talent, not any monetary reward, but I'm sure your readers would agree that a cash prize, however, small, is always welcome!'

To enter the competition, simply send in one original short story to: IWG, Dept 4011, FREEPOST, Ipswich, Suffolk IP2 6SN, UK. Your story should not exceed 3000 words, and your name, address and phone number should appear at the top of the first page. Enclose a separate self-addressed envelope if you want your story

to be returned. The text should preferably be typed, but a handwritten script is acceptable, as long as it's legible.

According to Sam, it's IWG policy to make every effort to discover new talent. 'Old or young, male or female, science fiction writers or romantic writers, or basically any kind of fiction writer – we're especially interested in receiving stories from people who haven't yet got their work in print. And anyone who's good enough to win a prize might find they can establish themselves as a writer and eventually earn a reasonable living from writing – we've seen it happen time and time again.'

All the stories entered for the competition will also be considered for possible publication in the IWG's collections of fiction, which are published at two-yearly intervals. The author of each story chosen for publication will receive a single extra payment, in addition to any prize money. Previous IWG collections have attracted media attention and some of the stories have been the subject of radio and television discussions.

I spoke to Billy Murray, a writer who was lucky enough – or talented enough – to win a prize two years ago. How had winning affected him? 'Well, people suddenly

➤

45 get interested in you, that's for sure,' he said, 'but they're hardly likely to become your best friends.' And the prize money? 'I can't tell you where that went. I certainly didn't end up any richer, and I don't reckon it made me a better writer! What I do recall, though, was the way I 50 began to feel differently about the whole writing thing – better, happier about the way I do it, less likely to keep questioning my approach.' What would he say to aspiring writers? 'I'd say to anyone out there wondering, should I have a go at writing – yes, go for it! What's there to lose? And there's no point in putting it off until you get a good 55 idea – just get started. I write my thoughts down in a diary every night, but that doesn't work for everybody. You must get some words on to paper, though – find a slot in the day that suits you and stick to it. And read back what you've written, and think about it.' 60

**1** How does Sam Payne feel about this year's competition?
- **A** impressed by the standard of entries so far
- **B** pleased with the generous prize money
- **C** glad that some different writers can take part
- **D** proud of the well-known authors who are entering

**2** If you wish to enter the competition, you should make sure that
- **A** your story is over 3000 words.
- **B** your story is all your own idea.
- **C** you put your contact details on a separate page.
- **D** you send your script to the IWG in San Francisco.

**3** Sam says the IWG is particularly hoping to encourage
- **A** unpublished writers.
- **B** writers who are short of money.
- **C** writers of a particular type of story.
- **D** younger writers.

**4** If the judges approve of your story, it may
- **A** appear in an annual collection.
- **B** be recorded and broadcast on radio.
- **C** earn a regular income for you.
- **D** be published with other authors' work.

**5** Billy Murray thinks that winning a prize in a previous competition
- **A** improved his writing technique.
- **B** widened his circle of friends.
- **C** benefited him financially.
- **D** gave him self-confidence.

**6** Billy Murray's advice to would-be writers is to
- **A** write for a fixed time every day.
- **B** wait for inspiration.
- **C** read other authors.
- **D** keep a diary.

# Unit 8

This is a **multiple-choice** task (see Unit 7). You need to use the skills of intensive reading and reading between the lines.

You are going to read a magazine article written by a wildlife photographer, Jenny Laverne. Choose the most appropriate answer (A, B, C or D) to each question.

## WORK IN THE WILD

I suppose you could say I've been passionate about wildlife since I was a child. One of my earliest memories is of getting keen on fishing in a stream near our house, and while I was
5 standing there waiting for the fish to bite, I'd start noticing all the wildlife. I'd rush home and tell my parents all about the animals and birds I'd seen. Later on I learnt a lot from my uncle, who's very knowledgeable about birds, and I watched every
10 wildlife series there was on TV. Then I bought my first camera, and a photographer was born!

I'm completely self-taught, as I don't believe you can learn a skill by sitting in a classroom. That said, friends and colleagues say you get a lot out
15 of attending courses – it just isn't my experience, so I wouldn't recommend it. Of course once you've learnt the basics, it might be fun to be a member of a photographic club, so you can work on projects together.

20 I'm busy all the time now that I'm better known, and I work spring, summer, autumn, winter, with hardly a break sometimes – not something I need or want to do, but I've got into the routine of it. I have to get the most out of each day, so I
25 often find myself making notes for articles, say, or editing images, maybe, while waiting in a hide for a bird to appear. I try to be patient, but luckily there's usually nobody to hear if I get cross and start muttering to myself!

30 The south-west is my home and that's where I take most of my photos. It's not that I mind driving or even flying further afield, I just feel there's such a diversity of subjects here, from red deer to field voles, so I'm lucky to have them on my doorstep. I
35 always ask my friends to tell me when they happen to spot an interesting or unusual animal if they're out walking, but they don't often remember! But I do sometimes get tip-offs from members of the public or wildlife organisations operating locally.

40 I've been working as a wildlife photographer for ten years now and have a pretty strong reputation, though I say so myself. I use the most sophisticated cameras and lenses I can get hold of, but that doesn't make me different from any other professional photographer. And I put in a
45 lot of hours, but again, that's something we all have to do. I think what I'm known for is being able to come up with exceptional images in adverse conditions. And wildlife is a popular area at the moment. Of course, it's not my only area of
50 expertise. I dabble in country sports, conservation projects and landscape shots as well.

I'm proud to say that almost all the subjects in my images are taken in the wild – under no circumstances are the animals put under any
55 stress or their habitat disturbed, and where necessary I obtain the appropriate licence. I have very occasionally photographed captive subjects, but only if a particular commission – a request from an owner, perhaps – requires this, or if I've
60 been asked to do so by the Secret World Animal Rescue Centre, which I'm happy to work with.

My range of clients varies from someone just wanting a picture to hang in their sitting room, to picture libraries and major wildlife charities.
65 I've been fortunate enough to win a couple of

→

international competitions. A while ago I spent ages checking the proofs of a book of what I think are my most beautiful photos – it's out
70 in the shops now, in fact. Something I haven't done, which would be fun, is to travel round the country showing a selection of my images at local art galleries and libraries. I like the idea of the contact with the public. But who knows what else will occur to me?
75

**1** What first gave Jenny an interest in wildlife?

    **A** her parents' enthusiasm for it

    **B** visiting her uncle's house in the country

    **C** taking up a particular hobby

    **D** her favourite television programme

**2** What does Jenny think the best way to learn photography is?

    **A** go on a course

    **B** teach yourself

    **C** learn from a friend

    **D** join a club

**3** Jenny says it is essential for her to

    **A** work during all four seasons.

    **B** be patient when she has to wait.

    **C** use her time effectively.

    **D** edit her images as soon as possible.

**4** Jenny says she prefers to take photos close to home because

    **A** she does not have to travel far.

    **B** there is a wide range of wildlife in her area.

    **C** she has useful links with local organisations.

    **D** her friends can suggest subjects to photograph.

**5** Jenny thinks she has a good reputation because she

    **A** concentrates on wildlife alone.

    **B** uses top-of-the-range equipment.

    **C** works harder than other photographers.

    **D** produces excellent pictures even in poor weather.

**6** What does Jenny try to avoid doing?

    **A** photographing animals in captivity

    **B** getting a licence to photograph wildlife

    **C** working for an animal rescue centre

    **D** relying on commissioned work for her income

**7** What is Jenny hoping to do in the future?

    **A** take an exhibition of her photos on tour

    **B** publish a book of her best pictures

    **C** gain international recognition

    **D** get her photos accepted by picture libraries

# Unit 9

This is a **multiple-choice** task (see Unit 7). You need to use the skills of intensive reading and reading between the lines.

You are going to read a newspaper article about coincidences. Choose the most appropriate answer (A, B or C) to each question.

## IS LIFE REALLY JUST A GAME OF CHANCE?

**As Sue Carpenter reports, there could be powerful paranormal forces at work.**

What are the chances of landing in a country of 20 million people and meeting someone, with
5 whom you had absolutely no prior connection, who turns out to be a relative you never knew you had? An extraordinary coincidence? Or something more? That was exactly what happened to a friend, Clare, ten years ago.
10 She and I were travelling through Australia and met up with friends of my brother's – Rob and his wife Jenny – for dinner. Small talk revealed that Jenny and Clare both had relatives who were fruit farmers in the south.
15 Then they discovered the greatest coincidence of all. Jenny and Clare, who had never met or even heard of one another before, were second cousins.

Coincidences have fascinated me ever since
20 that day in Sydney. Could it be possible that there is some unknown force pulling people or events together? When we really need something and out of the blue it comes to us, have we willed it to happen? When an old
25 friend rings up just as we're about to call them, are we sending out telepathic signals?

Recent research has thrown up some fascinating ideas on coincidences – and the new thinking is that they are much more than just a matter
30 of chance. Statisticians would argue that many apparently astounding incidents are more likely to occur than we would think. The probability of two people among 50 sharing a birthday is 97 per cent. And for every one-in-

a-million chance event, such as the collision 35 of motorcyclist Frederick Chance with driver Frederick Chance in Worcestershire in 1969, what of the 999,999 times it doesn't happen? In their *Encyclopaedia of the Unexplained*, however, Jenny Randles and Peter Hough 40 suggest that driving forces at the subconscious level can make a person be in a certain place at a certain time. Our inner minds guide us through a series of actions that lead us to the point where the 'coincidence' occurs.          45

There have been many apparently telepathic incidents. Sailor Chay Blyth's wife was dining at a restaurant, while her husband was thousands of miles away, braving the ocean in a catamaran. Suddenly she was overcome 50 with nausea and knew something was wrong. At that very moment, she later discovered, her husband's boat had capsized.

Last year I was on another long trip abroad, when an astonishing coincidence occurred. My 55 travelling companion, Lucy, had been thinking about her ex-boyfriend, Henry Slack. As we looked around a hotel in Zanzibar, enter Henry and friend, who had, quite independently, organised a fortnight's holiday there. It was 60 almost as if Lucy had conjured him up by the power of her thoughts.

People frequently report a sudden urge to contact someone close to them just before that person dies – although they have no 65 conscious knowledge of the impending death. As a trainee officer at Sandhurst, John Dawes woke up one night and told his wife that, in his dream, his mother had been trying to give him the combination of her safe. Next morning, his brother rang to tell him their mother had died. Just before passing away, she had tried to mouth the combination numbers of her safe.

Jenny Randles maintains that even non-personal twists of fate are linked on a level where space and time do not exist. Consider this case, for instance. In 1981, British Rail received a call from a woman who had had a vision of a fatal train crash, involving engine number 47216. Two years later, an identical accident happened – to train 47299. A trainspotter noticed, however, that this was not the train's original number. So impressed had BR been by the call that they had tried to avert disaster by changing the train's number – from 47216 to 47299.

**1** The writer says that her friend Clare
  **A** went to Australia to visit a cousin.
  **B** found an unexpected family connection.
  **C** met some friends by chance on a journey.

**2** What does the writer suggest about coincidences in paragraph 2?
  **A** They are purely imaginary.
  **B** They have held a lifelong interest for her.
  **C** They may be caused by something more than chance.

**3** The writer mentions the two men called Frederick Chance to show that
  **A** their names were invented.
  **B** they will probably never meet again.
  **C** their accident was an unlikely event.

**4** Jenny Randles and Peter Hough think the human subconscious may cause people
  **A** to take certain steps.
  **B** to avoid coincidences.
  **C** to be aware of the time.

**5** The wife of the sailor Chay Blyth felt sick because
  **A** she was not used to sailing.
  **B** she had eaten something bad.
  **C** she was sympathetic to her husband's situation.

**6** When Henry Slack arrived in Zanzibar, he came
  **A** to take a break from work.
  **B** in response to Lucy's invitation.
  **C** as one of the writer's group of friends.

**7** What is the point of John Dawes' story about his dream?
  **A** He regretted not saying goodbye to his mother.
  **B** He was aware of his dying mother's message.
  **C** He was able to open his mother's safe and get her money.

**8** British Rail changed the train's number because
  **A** a trainspotter had noticed it.
  **B** they thought the woman's story might be true.
  **C** it was hoped a second accident could be avoided.

# Unit 10

This is a **multiple-choice** task (see Unit 7). You need to use the skills of intensive reading and reading between the lines.

You are going to read an extract from *My Early Life* by Winston Churchill. Choose the most appropriate answer (A, B C or D) to each question.

My brother and I were sent this summer by our parents for a so-called walking tour of Switzerland, with a tutor. I need hardly say we travelled
5 by train so far as the money lasted. The tutor and I climbed mountains. We climbed the Wetterhorn and Monte Rosa. The spectacle of the sunrise striking the peaks of the Bernese
10 Oberland is a marvel of light and colour unsurpassed in my experience. I longed to climb the Matterhorn, but this was not only too expensive but held by the tutor to be too dangerous.
15 All this prudence, however, might easily have been upset by an incident which happened to me in the lake of Lausanne. I record this incident that it might be a warning to others.

20 I went for a row with another boy a little younger than myself. When we were more than a mile from the shore, we decided to have a swim, pulled off our clothes, jumped into the water
25 and swam about in great delight. When we had had enough, the boat was perhaps one hundred yards away. A breeze had begun to stir the waters. The boat had a small red awning over
30 its stern seats. This awning acted as a sail by catching the breeze. As we swam towards the boat, it drifted farther off. After this happened several times we had perhaps halved
35 the distance. But meanwhile the breeze was freshening and we both, especially my companion, began to be tired.

Up to this point no idea of danger had crossed my mind. The sun played 40 upon the sparkling blue waters; the wonderful panorama of mountains and valleys, the gay hotels and villas still smiled. But now I saw Death as near as I believe I have ever seen 45 him. He was swimming in the water at our side, whispering from time to time in the rising wind which continued to carry the boat away from us at about the same speed we could swim. No 50 help was near. Unaided, we could never reach the shore.

I was not only an easy, but a fast swimmer, having represented my House at Harrow* when our team 55 defeated all comers. I now swam for my life. Twice I reached within a yard of the boat and each time a gust carried it just beyond my reach; but by a supreme effort I caught hold of 60 its side in the nick of time before a still stronger gust bulged the red awning again. I scrambled in, and rowed back for my companion who, though tired, had not apparently realised the 65 dull yellow glare of mortal peril that had so suddenly played around us. I said nothing to the tutor about this serious experience; but I have never forgotten it.

*Harrow: a famous school in England

56

1 The writer uses the expression 'so-called' to describe the walking tour because
  A the tutor walked, while the writer and his brother went by train.
  B they were all supposed to be travelling by train, not on foot.
  C they only walked when they ran out of money.
  D it was a climbing trip rather than a walking tour.

2 The writer didn't climb the Matterhorn because
  A he thought it would take too long.
  B the risks were considered too great.
  C his parents couldn't afford the expense.
  D the tutor had been warned not to attempt it.

3 The writer says he is telling us this anecdote in order to
  A show how cautious he was.
  B describe his holiday in Lausanne.
  C explain how his character has developed.
  D prevent other people from getting into difficulties.

4 What did the two boys do on the lake?
  A They swam all round the lake and rowed back.
  B They dived into the water in their swimsuits.
  C They rowed some way and then swam.
  D They sailed out into the middle of it for a swim.

5 What mistake did the boys make?
  A They didn't realise the boat would move away from them.
  B They had no idea they had swum so far from the boat.
  C They didn't know the lake had a strong current.
  D They were unaware of the coldness of the breeze.

6 Who or what does 'He' refer to in line 46?
  A death
  B a ghost
  C the tutor
  D the writer's brother

7 Which of these statements is true?
  A The boat was drifting towards the writer.
  B The boys were unable to swim to the shore.
  C The writer found it impossible to reach the boat.
  D The other boy was exhausted and frightened.

8 How did the writer react to the experience on the lake?
  A He felt proud of saving the other boy's life.
  B He was afraid his parents might be angry.
  C He thought it was an unimportant incident.
  D He became aware of some of life's dangers.

# Unit 11

You are going to read an extract from *Adventure in Two Worlds* by A.J. Cronin. Choose the most appropriate answer (A, B, C or D) to each question.

Having emphatically declared before my entire household that I *would* write a novel – tacitly implying, of course, that it was the fault of *every* other
5 member of the household that I had not written twenty novels – I found myself faced with the unpleasant necessity of justifying my rash remarks. All I could do was to retire, with a show of
10 courage and deep purpose, to the top attic of the house, which had been at once selected as 'the room for Daddy to write in'. Here I was confronted by a square pine table, by a pile of twopenny
15 exercise books, and a dictionary.

It was the morning following our arrival. Amazingly, for that latitude, the sun shone. Our little dinghy danced entrancingly at anchor on
20 the loch, waiting to be rowed. My car stood in the garage, waiting to be driven. The trout in the river lay head to tail, waiting to be caught. The hills stood fresh and green, waiting to be
25 climbed. And I – I stood at the window of the little upstairs room. Wincingly, I looked at the sun, the loch, the boat, the car, the river and the mountains; then sadly turned and sat down before
30 my pine table, my exercise books and my dictionary. 'What a fool you are,' I said to myself gloomily. How often during the next three months was I to repeat the assertion – each time with
35 stronger adjectives.

But in the meantime I was going to begin. Firmly I opened the first exercise book, firmly I jogged my fountain pen out of its habitual inertia. Firmly I
40 poised that pen and lifted my head for inspiration.

It was a pleasant view through that narrow window: a long green field ran down to a bay of the loch. I thought
45 I might contemplate the scene for a minute or two before settling down to work. I contemplated. Then somebody knocked at the door and said, 'Lunchtime'. I started, and searched
50 hopefully for my glorious beginning, only to find that the exercise book still retained its blank virginity.

I rose and went downstairs, and I carved the mutton glumly. My two
55 young sons, removed by their nurse to a remote distance in order that they might on no account disturb the novelist, had returned in high spirits. The younger, aged four, now
60 lisped breezily: 'Finished your book yet, Daddy?' The elder, always of a corrective tendency, affirmed with the superior wisdom of his two additional years: 'Don't be silly. Daddy's only half finished.' Whereupon their mother
65 smiled upon them reprovingly: 'No, dears, Daddy can only have written a chapter or two.'

**1** Why did the narrator feel he had to start writing a novel?

    **A** He was competing with other writers in his family.

    **B** He thought it would bring in some much-needed money.

    **C** He wanted to contradict people who said he couldn't do it.

    **D** He had told his family he was going to write one.

**2** How did he feel when he stood at the attic window?

    **A** impatient for a change in the weather

    **B** depressed at the thought of the task ahead

    **C** surprised by the sight of his boat

    **D** disappointed by the scenery

**3** What happened during the morning?

    **A** He found it easy to get ideas.

    **B** He wrote the beginning of the novel.

    **C** He looked at the view out of the window.

    **D** He made notes for the first chapter, then lost them.

**4** What does 'I started' mean (line 49)?

    **A** I began to write at once.

    **B** I looked fixedly at the paper.

    **C** I stood up straight.

    **D** I jumped up in surprise.

**5** What did the narrator's wife think about his writing?

    **A** He was sure to be making some progress.

    **B** Her sons had a good understanding of his work.

    **C** It was fortunate he was able to write fairly fast.

    **D** It was a pity he had to spend so much time writing.

**6** The author's tone in the final paragraph is

    **A** objective.

    **B** enthusiastic.

    **C** humorous.

    **D** regretful.

**7** The narrator shows himself to be

    **A** proud of his abilities.

    **B** aware of his faults.

    **C** determined and hardworking.

    **D** cheerful and sociable.

**8** What would an appropriate title for this extract be?

    **A** Pressure to Achieve

    **B** A Family Holiday

    **C** Three Satisfying Months

    **D** Self-improvement

Section
3

# Gapped Texts

# Unit 12

You are going to read part of an article about Edward Jenner. Six sentences have been removed from the article. Choose from the sentences A – G the one which fits each gap. There is one extra sentence.

## JENNER'S CONTRIBUTION TO WORLD HEALTH

Smallpox is an acute, highly infectious disease, producing high fever and a pinkish rash of spots which, when they dry up, leave ugly scars on the skin. ⬚ 1 It was not until 1980
5　that the World Health Organisation declared that the disease was eradicated, after the final recorded case in Somalia in 1977.

Over two hundred years ago the English physician Edward Jenner discovered the
10　process of vaccination, which eventually offered reliable protection and caused smallpox to disappear completely. ⬚ 2 Here he saw people suffering both from smallpox and from cowpox, a weaker, much less dangerous
15　form of infection, frequently found in cows. He made the interesting observation that the local country people who caught cowpox because of their daily contact with cattle did not catch smallpox, even if close friends and
20　family were infected. ⬚ 3 This process was called vaccination, from vacca, the Latin word for cow.

Although other studies were being carried out elsewhere in Britain during the eighteenth century, Jenner made the clinical breakthrough, 25 and the immunity he provided against one of history's most terrifying diseases brought him fame and fortune. ⬚ 4 He was also given the freedom of the City of London in 1805, an honour not lightly granted. He died 30 in 1823.

⬚ 5 By this time, vaccination had become a compulsory part of many countries' public health programmes. It may seem surprising that Jenner's great discovery was 35 not fully exploited at the time. ⬚ 6

In the village of Berkeley in Gloucestershire, where Edward Jenner used to live, there is a museum which aims to remind us of this English physician's pioneering achievement. 40 The lives of millions of people have been saved by this one man's careful observation and clinical work.

**A** This can be partly explained by the fact that complete eradication required a concerted effort from all countries.

**B** By experimenting on local people, therefore, Edward Jenner was able to prove, in 1796, that injections of the cowpox virus could provide protection against smallpox.

**C** He was paid generous sums by the government when the authorities realised the importance of his achievement.

**D** After a lifetime of hard work, Jenner finally retired to the country, still hoping for the recognition he felt he had earned.

**E** For centuries it killed rich and poor alike, spreading fast when it took hold in an area, and often seriously disfiguring or blinding those sufferers who escaped death.

**F** Smallpox was not finally wiped out, however, until over a century later.

**G** Jenner was born in 1749 and, after studying medicine, lived and worked as a doctor in a small village in rural Gloucestershire.

## VOCABULARY CHECK

Which words do you want to remember? Write them down.

_____

_____

_____

Find adjectives in the text which mean:

**a** *easily passed on to other people* _____

**b** *unpleasant-looking* _____

**c** *risky* _____

**d** *frightening* _____

Find verbs in the text which mean:

**e** *get rid of completely* _____

**f** *give (an honour)* _____

**g** *make use of* _____

**h** *help someone remember* _____

# Unit 13

 This is a **gapped-text** task (see Unit 12). You need to use the skills of skimming and intensive reading.

You are going to read an article about a village in Canada. Seven sentences have been removed from the article. Choose from the sentences A – H the one which fits each gap. There is one extra sentence.

## THE VILLAGE THAT VANISHED

It isn't unusual to hear about a missing person, but in 1930 a whole village vanished – and it's still missing.

[ 1 ] Although it was an isolated spot, the Inuit people who lived there were frequently visited by trappers who swapped furs and joined them for meals. [ 2 ]

But in November 1930, when Joe decided to stop by the village for a visit, he immediately knew something was wrong. [ 3 ] He shouted a greeting but no one answered. Finally, he opened the doors to several of the huts and yelled for his friends. [ 4 ]

An hour-long search of the village showed that every inhabitant had disappeared. There were no signs of a struggle – pots of food sat over fires that had been cold for weeks. [ 5 ]

Kayaks had been left unattended for so long that waves had battered them. Rifles stood gathering dust. The Inuits' dogs were found dead from starvation, tied to wooden stumps. 25

The mystery deepened when LaBelle searched his friends' cemetery where bodies were customarily covered with rocks. One grave had been opened and the body exhumed*. Stealing a body, 30 LaBelle knew, was taboo for an Inuit. [ 6 ]

The Royal Canadian Mounted Police investigated LaBelle's report of the village that had disappeared. [ 7 ] 35 Months of detective work, including interviews with other tribes in the area, never turned up a clue to explain what had happened.

* *exhumed*: dug up, removed

**A** Despite their reputation of 'always getting their man', the Mounties were puzzled as to how and why thirty Inuits had vanished in the middle of winter.

**B** The first thing was that all the doors were open.

**C** The village was located near Lake Angikuni, about five hundred miles north-west of the Royal Canadian Mounted Police base at Churchill, Canada.

**D** A needle was still in some clothing that a woman had been mending.

**E** First of all, the dogs didn't bark.

**F** No one replied.

**G** Whoever had done the deed had stacked the grave stones in two piles – ruling out any possibility that an animal had uncovered the body.

**H** French-Canadian trapper Joe LaBelle, who had travelled through that part of the Canadian wilderness for about forty years, considered the folks who lived on Lake Angikuni old friends.

## VOCABULARY CHECK

Which words do you want to remember? Write them down.

_____

_____

_____

Without looking back at the text, can you explain these words?

**a** *vanished* _____

**b** *swapped* _____

**c** *battered* _____

**d** *starvation* _____

**e** *taboo* _____

**f** *reputation* _____

**g** *stacked* _____

# Unit 14

This is a **gapped-text** task (see Unit 12). You need to use the skills of skimming and intensive reading.

You are going to read a text about the writer Dylan Thomas. Seven sentences have been removed from the text. Choose from the sentences A – H the one which fits each gap. There is one extra sentence.

## DYLAN THOMAS

Dylan Marlais Thomas was born in Swansea in Wales in 1914. His parents had been brought up in the Welsh-speaking countryside and, although they taught their son to speak only English, he grew up surrounded by the culture and speech of South Wales, which were to play an important part in his work. His mother took him to chapel but his father read him Shakespeare instead. **1**
He was soon diagnosed with asthma, and because of these problems he was worried about his health all his life.

When he was as young as eight he started writing poetry, and his work appeared in his school magazine. Even as a teenager he was convinced he would die young. So his view was that he might as well enjoy life to the full, however short it was going to be. He started chain-smoking at fifteen and later took to drinking heavily. He showed absolutely no interest in any school subject except English, which he was extremely good at. **2**

He got a job as reporter on the *South Wales Daily Post*, but left after fifteen months, and had no further regular salaried employment. Still living at home, he did some acting at the Swansea Little Theatre for an amateur theatrical company. **3**

In 1933 he visited London and made some useful publishing contacts, sending work to various journals. In 1934 he went to live there, and published two books of poetry. Two years later he met his future wife, Caitlin Macnamara, with whom he had a long-lasting, passionate and stormy relationship. **4**

He was now becoming famous, and made his first radio broadcast. However, he became extremely depressed when he failed his medical test and was rejected for active service in World War II. One of his notable characteristics was a quite amazing disregard for the practicalities of day-to-day life. **5** In addition to his worries about his health, he was always short of money, as he seemed to spend it so fast. Then in 1948 there was a disastrous discovery. **6**

Partly to economise, Dylan and Caitlin returned to Wales and settled in the village of Laugharne. They had three children by now, and this was the poet's final really productive phase, including the writing of his radio play *Under Milk Wood*.

**7** But, inevitably, exhaustion, illness and the effects of drinking too much took their toll, and on 9th November 1953 Dylan Thomas died in New York at the age of thirty-nine, having collapsed a few days earlier.

**A** This was a very important time for his writing because, in those few years of living at home after leaving school, he wrote one of his best-known poems.

**B** For much of his childhood, serious lung problems kept him confined to bed.

**C** But critics have only recently come to appreciate the fire and originality of his writing.

**D** Other people often had to take on his responsibilities, but even so, the last years of his life were ruined by ill health and financial difficulties.

**E** The authorities found out that Dylan Thomas had paid no tax at all during his life and, as a result, he was in debt to the tax office and others right up to his death.

**F** He was delighted to achieve his ambition of going to America, to give talks and readings around the country, in the early 1950s.

**G** Neither had any idea about managing money, but they were deeply in love all their lives, despite the difficulties they had to cope with.

**H** He left school at sixteen without passing any exams, and was only interested in poetry.

## VOCABULARY CHECK

Which words do you want to remember? Write them down.

_____

_____

_____

Find verbs which mean:

**a** *name a medical problem* _____

**b** *smoke heavily* _____

**c** *save money* _____

**d** *make somewhere your permanent home* _____

Find phrases which mean:

**e** *have a short life* _____

**f** *as well as* _____

**g** *ruin someone's health* _____

**h** *owing money* _____

# Unit 15

This is a **gapped-text** task (see Unit 12). You need to use the skills of skimming and intensive reading.

You are going to read an information leaflet for drivers. Seven sentences have been removed from the text. Choose from the sentences A – H the one which fits each gap. There is one extra sentence.

## THE M25 MOTORWAY

Drivers intending to use the M25 Motorway in Surrey need to remember that there are roadworks in both directions between Junctions 6 and 10 (the Godstone
5 to Wisley section). ☐1☐ A compulsory 50-mph speed limit has been imposed throughout the whole length of the roadworks, and motorists who exceed this limit will be prosecuted.
10 ☐2☐ The speed limit is necessary in order to keep traffic running smoothly and safely through the roadworks. In addition, the workforce needs to be protected, and this cannot reliably be
15 done without a 50-mph limit.

There will usually be three lanes open in the daytime in each direction, but at night certain lanes will be closed to traffic. ☐3☐ Calls are charged at 3p a
20 minute from landlines; calls from mobiles usually cost more.

The roadworks have been undertaken to add extra lanes in each direction between Junctions 6 and 10, one of the busiest
25 stretches of the motorway. This is being done to aid traffic flow at peak times and to reduce accidents. New road signs and lighting systems are also being installed, to improve safety. However, we are very
30 conscious of the impact a motorway can have on local residents, on the environment, and on wildlife habitats. ☐4☐
Please note that emergency telephones will not be operating on this stretch, and 35 that there will therefore be a free recovery service throughout the roadworks, in order to keep the traffic lanes clear. ☐5☐ A breakdown truck will arrive to tow you to the nearest garage, free 40 of charge.

Here is some advice for the motorist on this section of the M25:

- Allow plenty of time for your journey and avoid the area in the rush hour if 45 you can.

- Keep to the speed limit to avoid the risk of prosecution.

- ☐6☐

- Get into the correct lane in good time 50 and follow the direction signs.

- There may be delays caused by traffic build-up, so you might prefer to travel by train. ☐7☐

You can find out more about the progress 55 of the roadworks by ringing the real-time traffic information line on 08700 660 115 or by accessing our website at www.highways.gov.uk. We hope you will not be greatly inconvenienced, and 60 we ask for your full co-operation.

**A** Information is available on this line from 7 a.m. to 11 p.m. only.

**B** Ring 08457 48 49 50 for information on train routes and timetables, or access the www.nationalrail.co.uk website.

**C** As a result, every effort is being made to minimise any negative effects, with the provision of noise barriers, grassy slopes and natural vegetation.

**D** This particular section is undergoing widening work and improvements to the surface, which started in May and will continue to the end of the year.

**E** Drive extra carefully through the roadworks and keep your distance from all other vehicles.

**F** For details of lane closures, drivers can phone the information line on 08457 50 40 30 at any time.

**G** So if you break down, do not set off on foot to try to find a phone, but turn on your hazard lights, get out on the passenger side, and wait in a safe place near your vehicle.

**H** In order to catch offenders, police speed checks, using speed cameras, will be in operation.

## VOCABULARY CHECK

Which words do you want to remember? Write them down.

_____

_____

_____

Without looking back at the text, can you explain these words?

**a** *prosecuted* _____

**b** *workforce* _____

**c** *reliably* _____

**d** *impact* _____

**e** *habitats* _____

**f** *tow* _____

# Unit 16

This is a **gapped-text** task (see Unit 12). You need to use the skills of skimming and intensive reading.

You are going to read a text about the painter Vincent Van Gogh. Seven sentences have been removed from the text. Choose from the sentences A – H the one which fits each gap. There is one extra sentence.

## VINCENT VAN GOGH

One of the world's best-known painters, Vincent Van Gogh, was born in Zundert in the Netherlands in 1853. [1]
He began his working life in 1869 as an employee of the Goupil Art Gallery, where his brother Theo also worked for a time. Vincent stayed with the gallery for seven years, working at branches in The Hague, London and Paris. [2]
It was the latter subject he decided to concentrate on for a while, and so from December 1878 to July 1879 he worked in a coal-mining district in Belgium as a preacher.

It was on his return to his native country that he gave himself the task of perfecting his drawing, but he also painted with watercolours and later in oils. Known as the Dutch period, this residence in the Netherlands produced works depicting misery and despair. [3] His subjects, ordinary working men and women, were portrayed sympathetically and without exaggeration. *The Potato Eaters*, painted in 1885, is a famous work dating from this period. Later, in the mental hospital at Saint-Rémy, Van Gogh remembered it with affection. [4]

For three months (December 1885 to February 1886) Van Gogh was in Antwerp, where his artistic development continued.

He became more interested in colour, influenced not only by the paintings of Rubens on show in the museums, but also by the Japanese prints he had begun to collect. It was here that he started his cycle of self-portraits. [5] His works of this period are full of light and feeling, marked by lively brush-strokes and fresh colours, mostly whites, pinks and blues.

In February 1888 he left Paris for Arles, in the south of France, hoping to find the strong light and bright colour which other artists had talked so much about. He soon abandoned Impressionism and concentrated on evolving his own distinctive style. [6] The first signs of his subsequent illness had become apparent and, from this moment on, Van Gogh suffered from fits of insanity.

During his remaining eighteen months of life, he was in and out of hospital, but he continued to produce many fully developed works, some of which are now considered masterpieces. [7] But in the end, fearing another breakdown, Van Gogh put an end to his existence by shooting himself. Illness and loneliness had made his life too hard to bear, but he left behind an impressive legacy of creative artistic achievement.

**A** However, it was when he moved to Paris in February 1886 that he met other artists and experimented with a form of Impressionism.

**B** His final few months were spent in the home of a Dr Gachet, who took him in and cared for him.

**C** Although he showed a talent for drawing from the age of nine, he did not become aware of his artistic vocation until 1880, at the relatively late age of 27.

**D** 'I have tried to make it clear,' he wrote, 'how these people, eating their potatoes under the lamplight, have dug the earth with those very hands they put in the dish; and so the painting speaks of manual labour and how they have honestly earned their food.'

**E** Then he started an apprenticeship in a bookshop at Dordrecht, while at the same time studying theology.

**F** The French painter Paul Gauguin came to Arles at Van Gogh's invitation, but Vincent's first experience of communal artistic life ended with a crisis, when he tried to attack Gauguin, then cut off part of his own ear.

**G** These reflected his experiences in the coal-mining area, when he had been continually surrounded by poverty and unhappiness.

**H** Surrounded by friends and close family right up to the end, he passed away, after a lifetime of struggle and effort.

## VOCABULARY CHECK

Which words do you want to remember? Write them down.

_____

_____

_____

Find adjectives which mean:

**a** *where you were born* _____

**b** *related to art* _____

**c** *different from other people's* _____

**d** *working with your hands* _____

Find nouns which mean:

**e** *a warm feeling like love* _____

**f** *an excellent work of art* _____

**g** *something you leave behind when you die* _____

**h** *being very poor* _____

# Multiple Matching

# Unit 17

A **multiple-matching** task requires you to read a number of questions or statements and to find the answers in a long text or series of shorter texts, by matching the questions with the correct section of text. The task focuses on detail and specific information, as well as opinions and attitudes expressed in the text.

Here are some tips for dealing with this:

- First read the questions or statements carefully.
- Scan the text(s) for the appropriate answers, looking for matching ideas.
- Identify the topic, source and register as you read the text(s).
- Use speed reading if time is short.

You are going to read some previews of television programmes. For questions 1 – 15, choose from the programmes (A – H). The programmes may be chosen more than once.

**Which programme(s)**

give you an insight into politics?  1 ☐  2 ☐

are concerned with health problems?  3 ☐  4 ☐

deal with international finance?  5 ☐  6 ☐

are on Friday evenings?  7 ☐  8 ☐

offers advice to the discriminating holidaymaker?  9 ☐

may be useful if you don't eat meat?  10 ☐

gives an update on scientific research?  11 ☐

cover aspects of history?  12 ☐  13 ☐

is a fictional, not factual, portrayal?  14 ☐

can help when you're planning outdoor activities?  15 ☐

**A  TRAVEL SHOW – Thursday 21.30**
Presenters Jan Fortune and Robbie Michaels go off the beaten track to introduce you to some of the world's most exciting and remote islands. This week – Tuvalu and Pitcairn.

**B  QUESTIONS IN THE HOUSE – Saturday 21.00**
The final episode in the drama serial set in the corridors of power. Will the President recover in time to prevent his rivals from overthrowing the government? Will society be able to survive the struggle between right and wrong? 'Incredibly close to real life' (*The Herald*); 'This could happen to us' (*Daily Observer*).

**C  GENDER BALANCE – Sunday 20.00**
Jacques Baudouin, Professor of Ancient Languages at the Sorbonne, explains the comparative roles of men and women in Ancient Rome, using data from recent archaeological finds near Pompeii to illustrate his ideas. This is one of the lectures by eminent speakers in the *Civilisation* series.

**D  INTO THE FUTURE – Friday 18.30**
Jake Mitchell reports on the first medical trials of a new type of cancer therapy in California, and Sophie Murdoch finds out the latest and most effective way of keeping salmon in good condition on fish farms.

**E  WHAT'S COOKING? – Tuesday 19.00**
Italian chef Giuseppe Bardolini shows us the secrets of Sicilian cuisine, while Paula Greene investigates vegetarian beliefs and recipes, and gives us ten tips for a low-cholesterol diet.

**F  NEWS AND WEATHER – Monday to Friday 21.00**
The latest news and business bulletins from around the world, with headlines, interviews with parliamentary candidates, regular feature stories, and global and local weather. Presenters: John Bateman and Cherry Singh.

**G  THE WAY IT WAS – Monday 21.30**
Simon Henton visits the royal palace of Versailles, as it used to be in the Sun King's time; an ancient monastery in Sussex, Michelham Priory, yields up its secrets to Maddie Hadley; and Alan Campbell spends a night in Scotland's oldest house, which has a famously visible ghost.

**H  MONEY MATTERS – Wednesday 18.00**
This weekly magazine programme covers all aspects of global business, including special reports from our correspondents and an analysis of important economic developments.

# Unit 18

This is a **multiple-matching** task (see Unit 17). You need to use the skills of scanning, identifying topic, source and register, and speed reading.

You are going to read some book reviews. For questions 1 – 15, choose from the books (A – H). The books may be chosen more than once.

**Which book(s)**

is recommended by an expert? **1** [     ]

is suitable for a child to read? **2** [     ]

deal with aspects of crime? **3** [     ] **4** [     ]

might give you ideas for a garden? **5** [     ] **6** [     ]

might serve as a useful checklist of recent events? **7** [     ]

is a biography? **8** [     ]

was not appreciated by the reviewer? **9** [     ]

may help you take responsibility for staying well? **10** [     ] **11** [     ]

is said to contain poor illustrations? **12** [     ]

includes elements of suspense? **13** [     ]

gives a detailed picture of society in a past era? **14** [     ]

includes illustrations by the author? **15** [     ]

**A  The Missing Diamond  £8.95**

Harriet Rosewall goes in pursuit of the international diamond smugglers who have stolen the most valuable jewel in the world. She doesn't seem to realise how determined they are, and how dangerous things will be for her if she continues her hunt. Luckily she has her faithful assistant, Jeff Banks, to help her. And this time Jeff is literally worth his weight in gold.

**B  Have a Heart  £11.95**

A new book reveals all you need to know about natural ways to relieve high blood pressure and reduce the risk of heart disease. It describes the lifestyle factors that may be making you vulnerable to a life-threatening illness, and gives you a number of techniques to combat them. Exercises and herbal medicines are also recommended.

**C  The Complete Guide to Your Body £15.95**

This hardback book describes the workings of the human body in great detail, with colour illustrations. It's invaluable for reference when you have a minor ailment, and is also a self-help manual for keeping healthy, without having to make frequent visits to the doctor. 'A most helpful, comprehensive work.' (*Dr E. Sims, British Medical Association*)

**D  Green Rules  £12.99**

Jackie Hargreaves, the TV horticultural expert, visits thirty homes round the country, from castles to cottages, and gives us detailed planting schemes for each one. She recommends plants for chalk and sand, for sun and shade, for north and south, for wet and dry soils, along with her trademark sketches, which readers are sure to find enjoyable.

**E  A Guide to South America  £8.50**

By far the worst of the bunch this week, this travel book makes miserable reading. Its information on public transport is inaccurate and the maps are confused and out of date. You would do better without it, despite its recommendations for cheap hotels and restaurants.

**F  Portrait of the Artist  £18.95**

A beautifully produced coffee-table book with many glossy colour photos, this describes the life of the painter Claude Monet, concentrating in particular on his life at Giverny, where he lived from 1883 right up to his death in 1926. There are many fascinating sketches and illustrations of his estate there, which he filled with rare plants, and views of the lake and waterlilies, which he painted so often.

**G  Pride and Prejudice  £4.95**

Jane Austen's great novel is now available in a shorter form, with the language adapted to a vocabulary limit of 2,500 words. Suitable for young readers, it evokes all the atmosphere of Austen's country house life, while being much more accessible. Other adaptations are planned in the same series.

**H  World Events  £9.95**

This is a round-up of all the most important happenings in the last year, from a global viewpoint. Disasters, wars, epidemics, political events, assassinations, massacres – they are all here, with highly sophisticated comment from experts on how and why they happened.

# Unit 19

This is a **multiple-matching** task (see Unit 17). You need to use the skills of scanning, identifying topic, source and register, and speed reading.

You are going to read some advertisements for holidays. For questions 1 – 15, choose from the advertisements (A – H). The advertisements may be chosen more than once.

**Which advertisement(s) mention(s)**

the chance to acquire a skill?  [1          ]

a need to power your own transport?  [2          ]

a warning about possible lack of comfort?  [3          ]

trips to wildlife reserves?  [4          ]

activities considered suitable for parents?  [5          ]

destinations still unspoilt by mass tourism?  [6          ] [7          ]

touring by bus?  [8          ] [9          ]

a high standard of accommodation?  [10          ]

an environment free from pollution?  [11          ]

do-it-yourself accommodation?  [12          ] [13          ]

the opportunity to sample interesting food?  [14          ]

an atmosphere not found anywhere else?  [15          ]

**A** *Departing every Sunday till October 6, from £489*

You are invited to experience the breathtaking beauty of Ireland on board one of our luxury coaches. Here is your chance to take in some of the wonderful West Coast scenery on a relaxing 8-day holiday. You will enjoy the unique ambience and traditional, slow pace of life which make Ireland so popular with holidaymakers of all ages.

**B** *A 2-week journey of discovery for the true traveller*

Travel with us in small groups in overland vehicles to explore the ancient country of Ethiopia. Visit royal palaces, island monasteries, medieval churches and rural villages. As most people haven't discovered Ethiopia yet, accommodation will be simple and road conditions may be poor in places. £2,185 including air fares and full board.

**C** *Prague to Venice by bike, £560 including air fare to Prague and 13 nights' camping*

It's about 800 miles from the Czech capital to Venice, and I did it in a fortnight, with 130 other cyclists. We rode through southern Bohemia, the Austrian mountains, a corner of Slovenia and part of the north Italian plain, our luggage carried for us in two large vans. Food was prepared by a mobile catering team while we put up our tents. Beautiful views, excellent organisation. Why don't you try it?

**D** *The real Crete, from £625 per person for 2 weeks*

The picturesque inland village of Stilos in north-western Crete has a small river that flows into the sea at nearby Kalives, with its beaches and traditional tavernas. The rustic charm of the area has not yet been wrecked by an invasion of holidaymakers, and you can relax and enjoy the local hospitality and attractive scenery.

**E** *Exploring the Coromandel area, return fare UK to New Zealand about £850*

Do you want natural beauty, fabulous scenery and bush walks? Do you want sandy beaches, clean water to bathe in and plenty of camp sites? Would you like to explore abandoned gold mines, go fishing or birdwatching? If you've answered yes to any of these, you should come to the Coromandel in New Zealand, where camping costs around £5 per night per person, and motel rooms are available for around £30 (double).

**F** *London to the Taj Mahal, 7 nights from £950*

Take advantage of our experience in the travel field and join our trip from London to Agra, visiting the beautiful 17th-century Taj Mahal, Old and New Delhi, and Jaipur. All hotels are 5 star, and you will be accompanied by our expert guides. Optional excursions include visits to the Bharatpur Bird Sanctuary and Keoladeo Ghana National Park.

**G** *Highland House Party, departing 25 May, 6 days from only £219*

A super holiday in beautiful Scotland. All this is included: travel by luxury coach, 5 nights half board, and daily excursions to lakes, castles and craft centres. Enjoy the whole range of Scottish entertainment, historic buildings and stunning scenery!

**H** *A coastal paradise, return fare £440 before August*

When you've been round Disney World in Orlando with the kids, what is there left to do? Plenty! Enjoy the fabulous beaches and chance to relax that Florida offers! Learn to sail at one of the sailing schools, go diving, take photos of the amazing mix of modern architectural styles, and taste the glorious variety of shellfish, fruit and vegetables on offer in the bustling markets and sophisticated restaurants.

# Unit 20

This is a **multiple-matching** task (see Unit 17). You need to use the skills of scanning, identifying topic, source and register, and speed reading.

You are going to read a magazine article about families' attitudes to eating. For questions 1 – 15, choose from the families (A – E). The families may be chosen more than once.

**Match each statement with the correct family/families.**

They're proud of their cooking.  | 1 | | 2 |

They have happy memories of childhood food.  | 3 |

They pay little attention to their food.  | 4 |

Their approach to food is based on tradition.  | 5 |

They're worried about eating certain types of food.  | 6 | | 7 |

They often eat separately.  | 8 |

They've changed their eating habits.  | 9 | | 10 |

Their social principles make them reject a particular food.  | 11 |

They take care to eat fresh vegetables.  | 12 |

Their lifestyle tends to dictate the way they eat.  | 13 | | 14 |

They make use of convenience foods.  | 15 |

# THE FOOD FILE

*What are your views on food? How important is it to you? How much time do you spend thinking about it, planning menus, preparing it and eating? Here's what some of you think.*

**A** **Sarah and Richard Thompson** eat only additive-free food that they cook at home. They've been doing this ever since their son Hugo was born. 'We didn't care what we ate before that,' admits Sarah. 'We used to eat all kinds of rubbish, junk food, takeaways, frozen meals ... But when you have a child you really become aware of how important food is. We believe you are what you eat, and who'd want to be a hamburger! It does take more time, of course, to do the shopping and prepare everything yourself. We buy fresh fish or meat, and organic fruit and things like salad and root veg every other day, and I do a lot of baking. It's very satisfying to know we're eating the right things, and everything tastes so much better.'

**B** **Peggy and Bill Colley** are retired now, and Bill tends to do most of the cooking, as Peggy is in a wheelchair. 'We don't eat as much as we used to,' he says. 'Neither of us has much appetite these days. I remember the Sunday lunch we used to have as kids – all of us round the big table with plates piled high with chicken and veg and roast potatoes, and then a pudding to follow! Oh, it was lovely, but I couldn't manage that now. No, Peggy and I often have cheese on toast, or a bit of soup, or something out of a packet. I'm not much of a cook really. It's too much bother to peel a lot of vegetables anyway.'

**C** **Daniel and Caroline Basson** both have high-flying jobs and lead a hectic life. 'I can't remember the last time we ate at home together in the week,' says Daniel. 'I usually have a meeting or something else on, so I tend to grab a bite in a handy bistro near the office. It's often a working meal, so I hardly notice what I'm eating. It could be pasta or salad, or occasionally a steak. And Caroline travels a lot for her job, so she's often away. She's not really bothered about her food either.'

**D** **Trevor and Sue Burke-Johnson** have both been vegetarians since their student days, and their children are too. They say there are lots of reasons why they don't eat meat. As Sue explains, 'We don't have complete confidence in modern methods of food production. Just how safe is meat these days? It could be full of hormones or other additives, which might affect our health. And then another thing is, what right have we got to take over so much of the planet for producing meat? Growing cereal takes up much less space, and developing countries manage very well with hardly any meat at all. Anyway, I couldn't bring myself to kill an animal, so I don't think I should expect anyone else to. I don't think we'll ever eat meat again.'

**E** **Henry Sutcliff** takes a rather different view. He lives with his two elderly sisters, **Ellen and Kate**, in the family home. He believes in eating meat every day. 'What was good enough for our parents is good enough for us. We all need protein, don't we? And I maintain you need three good meals a day, just to keep going. A cooked breakfast is important, too. You get tired and run-down if you don't eat properly. We really enjoy our food. My sisters do the cooking between them. They use good old-fashioned recipes, and I promise you, their cooking is wonderful!'

# Unit 21

This is a **multiple-matching** task (see Unit 17). You need to use the skills of scanning, identifying topic, source and register, and speed reading.

You are going to read part of a leaflet about the Empire State Building in New York. For questions 1 – 15, choose from the sections A – F. The sections may be chosen more than once.

**Which section mentions**

the material the entrance hall is made of? `1`

the subject of the building's works of art? `2`

the height of the building? `3`

the location of the viewing platforms? `4`

the material the outside is made of? `5`

the number of people who have visited the building? `6`

its whereabouts in New York? `7`

lights being used to enhance the appearance at certain times? `8`

the building's fame around the world? `9`

facilities designed for the comfort of the visitors? `10`

special consideration given to wildlife? `11`

an impressive visual contrast? `12`

the maximum extent of the view from the building? `13`

a painstaking approach during the process of building? `14`

a musical connection? `15`

# NEW YORK'S EMPIRE STATE BUILDING – 'THE CATHEDRAL OF THE SKIES'

A   New York's Empire State Building is an internationally known landmark which has been called 'the cathedral of the skies'. This iconic building of 103 floors soars 1454 feet (443 metres) into the atmosphere, offering unsurpassed views around the horizon, night or day, in wet weather or dry, to visitors from around the world. Tens of millions of people have marvelled at the breathtaking sights they have beheld from its two observatories.

B   Designed by the world-famous firm of architects, Shreve, Lamb & Harmon of New York City, and completed in 1931, the Empire State Building is centrally situated in the heart of Manhattan, where many other architecturally significant buildings are overlooked by this 'architectural splendor'.

The exterior of the building is made of Indiana limestone and granite trimmed with mullions of sparkling stainless steel, which reach from the sixth floor to the pinnacle. Whether seen in sunlight or moonlight, the tower glistens magnificently.

C   The 86th-floor observatory, at 1050 feet (320 metres), reached by high-speed automatic elevators, has both a glass-enclosed area, which is heated in winter and cooled in summer, and spacious outdoor promenades on all four sides of the building. High-powered binoculars are available on the promenades for the convenience of visitors at a minimal cost. A snack bar and souvenir counters are also located here.

Standing on the 102nd floor – 1250 feet (381 metres) above the bustling

streets below – one is reminded of the song 'On a Clear Day You Can See Forever'. Actually, on clear days visitors can see the surrounding countryside for distances of up to 80 miles, looking into the neighboring states of New York, New Jersey, Pennsylvania, Connecticut and Massachusetts.

D   The eight original art works in the lobby, entitled 'The Eight Wonders of the World', were created by artist Roy Sparkia and his wife Renee Nemorov. They have been a distinguished attraction in the entrance hall since their unveiling in 1963. Using a technique which permits the artist to paint with light as well as color, the subjects include the Seven Wonders of the Ancient World, as well as the Eighth Wonder of the Modern World – the actual Empire State Building.

E   The lobby of this impressive building is a work of art in itself. The marble came from Italy, France, Belgium and Germany. Experts combed these countries to obtain the most beautiful marble and, in one case, removed the contents of an entire quarry to ensure the right color and graining.

F   The upper 30 floors of the building are illuminated nightly from sunset to midnight, either in white or an appropriate color scheme to mark special events in the city. The lights remain switched off, however, when large numbers of migrating birds are flying in the vicinity, in spring and fall. The incomparable night view from the top of the Empire State Building is a fantasy of lights and stars sparkling and dancing against a panoramic background of darkness.

# Practice Tests

You are going to read an extract from the novel *Friends, Lovers, Chocolate* by Alexander McCall Smith, about a woman called Isabel Dalhousie. For questions 1 – 8, choose the most appropriate answer (A, B, C or D).

The note from Jamie was short and to the point. *I shall not be surprised*, he wrote, *if you do not wish to see me again. If I were you, I wouldn't. So all I can say is this: I should not have walked out of the St Honoré like that. It was childish and silly. I'm very sorry.*

5      'Dear Jamie,' she wrote in reply. 'If there is anybody with any apologising to do, it is me. I had intended to telephone you and tell you how sorry I am but I didn't get round to it in the excitement. But an apology is due from me and you are getting it. Your feelings for Cat are your affair and I have no business passing comment on them. I shall not do that again.
10    So please forgive me for telling you what to do when you hadn't asked for my advice in the first place.

       'There is one further thing. I am *very* pleased that you have decided not to go to London. London is all very well, in its place, which is four hundred miles or so south of Edinburgh. Londoners are perfectly agreeable people
15    – very cheerful, in spite of everything – but I'm sure that you are so much more appreciated in Edinburgh than you would be in London. I, for one, appreciate you, and I know that Grace does too, and then there are all those pupils of yours whose musicianship would take a dive were you to absent yourself. In short, we have all had a narrow escape.

20    'Does that sound selfish? Yes, it does to me. It sounds to me as if I am giving you all sorts of reasons to stay in Edinburgh while really only thinking of myself and how much I would miss your company if you were to go. So you must discount my advice on that score and do exactly as you wish, should a future opportunity arise. And I must do the same.
25    Although I have no desire to go anywhere, except for Western Australia, and the city of Mobile in Alabama, and Havana, and Buenos Aires, and …'

       She finished the letter, addressed it, and placed it on the hall table. Jamie would get her apology tomorrow and she would arrange to see him the day afterwards. She could ask him to bring some music and they would
30    go into the music room and she would play the piano while he sang and it became dark outside. The editor of the *Review of Applied Ethics* (at the piano) with her friend, Jamie (tenor). She thought to herself – and smiled at the thought – if one followed the well-ordered life one would start each day with the writing of one's letters of apology … She wondered for a
35    moment who else might be expecting an apology from her.

**1** In his note Jamie stresses that

   **A** he doesn't wish to see her again.

   **B** he is ashamed of what he did.

   **C** he is surprised at her response.

   **D** he will apologise if she asks him to.

**2** What is the first point Isabel makes in her reply?

   **A** There was no need for him to write to her.

   **B** She has been too busy to worry about their disagreement.

   **C** She appreciates being able to offer suggestions.

   **D** His feelings for the person called Cat do not interest her at all.

**3** What does 'it' in line 8 refer to ?

   **A** a reply

   **B** the excitement

   **C** an apology

   **D** the quarrel

**4** Isabel is pleased with Jamie's decision because she thinks that

   **A** London is near enough for Jamie to visit her.

   **B** Jamie would not find such good friends in London.

   **C** Edinburgh people are just as cheerful as Londoners.

   **D** There are disadvantages to living in both places.

**5** What does Isabel say in the paragraph beginning on line 20?

   **A** She hopes Jamie will take her advice.

   **B** She is thinking of what is best for Jamie.

   **C** She will soon get used to Jamie's absence.

   **D** She is aware of her real motives when replying to Jamie.

**6** Isabel refers to Western Australia, Mobile, Havana and Buenos Aires in lines 25 – 6 in order to show

   **A** the appeal of well-known destinations.

   **B** the variety of places she has planned to visit.

   **C** that what she has just written is not exactly true.

   **D** that she has decided to move away from Edinburgh.

**7** What is Isabel looking forward to in the final paragraph?

   **A** organising her life more carefully from now on

   **B** gaining musical instruction from Jamie

   **C** resuming her friendship with Jamie

   **D** ensuring she apologises more often in future

**8** In the letter as a whole, what is Isabel's tone?

   **A** emotional

   **B** sincere

   **C** amused

   **D** impersonal

# Part 2

You are going to read some advice on walking and climbing in wintry conditions. Seven sentences have been removed from the text. Choose from the sentences A – H the one which fits each gap. There is one extra sentence.

## WINTER WARNING

*Few people know more about walking than Countrywide Holidays, whose guesthouses offer guided walking programmes throughout the year.* | 9 |

Walking in the cold, short days of winter is a different world from the
5   warm, long days of summer, especially in the mountains. | 10 |
This is particularly true in winter, when a slight breeze over snowcapped hills has a drastic chill factor. Conditions can deteriorate within minutes to blow arctic blizzards over the mountain tops, requiring winter clothing, precise navigation and awareness of the potential dangers.

10   You will see how quickly blowing snow can cover the tracks of other walkers, and mist can easily hide cairns* and waymarks. | 11 | In this potentially dangerous situation, the use of winter equipment may be required, or diversions made to your route. And bear in mind that the careful use of winter equipment such as ice axes and crampons, or having
15   to find an alternative route, may hinder progress and take time.

| 12 | It eats into your energy. To cope with the low temperatures the body burns up huge amounts of reserves. Energy is also required in greater quantities to keep walking in snow and against strong winds.
| 13 | This can easily result in an accident. In addition, hot drinks
20   and high energy food are vital, as well as being a great comfort on a cold mountain.

Dusk comes early on winter days and catches out many an unwary walker. So favourite walks completed easily in summer conditions may have to be rushed or cut short. Changes in temperature, patches of ice or
25   streams in flood can delay walkers, who may be overtaken by nightfall.
| 14 |

Some people find winter walking the very best there is – but it demands a greater respect for and knowledge of the mountains and increased preparation and fitness. | 15 | Take extra clothing, food, hot drinks,
30   survival bag, torch and winter equipment which you should already know how to use. Leave full details of your route, escape route and ETA*, and if in doubt go with an experienced guide.

*cairns: piles of stones as landmarks
*ETA: expected time of arrival

**A** Furthermore, thick cloud, mist and dark skies can draw darkness in even earlier.

**B** So check local weather forecasts, plan ahead within your capabilities, and plan alternative routes in case of earlier descent.

**C** Tiredness and fatigue are the eventual result of the increased effort.

**D** Cold is a killer.

**E** Your route can become perilous, with ice hidden under the fresh snow.

**F** Don't forget to tell someone where you are planning to go.

**G** Whether you're planning a ramble on the North Yorkshire moors or the Lakeland fells, the following advice from CH is based on a century of walking experience.

**H** Remember that weather conditions are always variable in the hills.

# Part 3

You are going to read part of a magazine article about education. For questions 16 – 30, choose from the people (A – E). The people may be chosen more than once.

**Who implies or states the following opinions?**

Children benefit from learning basic skills at an early age. `16`

Practice rather than theory is the best way of learning. `17`

Testing students is best done by means of written exams. `18`

Modern technology can be a problem for uneducated people. `19`

The main aim of education is to help students find a job. `20` `21`

Teachers should encourage personal development. `22`

Pupils and students suffer from the pressure of academic work. `23` `24`

The majority of undergraduates are in need of financial help. `25`

Acquiring general knowledge is pointless. `26`

Teachers should be treated with politeness and consideration. `27`

Discipline is an important part of school life. `28`

The purpose of education is to ensure that students attain certain levels of ability. `29`

There are more educational opportunities now than in the past. `30`

# THE HAPPIEST DAYS OF YOUR LIFE?

**So what do *you* think education's all about? Let's hear your views! Here are some of our readers' comments so far.**

**A** **Sharon Woolford** left school at 16 because she just wanted to earn some money. Now she's a waitress. Does she regret leaving early? 'No, I don't. I enjoy my job. I think schools should prepare you for work, and mine didn't. We spent all our time on projects, and learning useless facts. It seemed such a waste of time somehow. Who wants to know what the longest river in Europe is? *I* don't!'

**B** **Simon Taggart** is a solicitor, and says he worked hard at school because he knew he wanted to get somewhere in life. 'I passed all my exams, got into university and qualified as a solicitor. People say exams are stressful – well, they are, but I think they're necessary. They're the only reliable way of finding out how good students are at their subjects. And that's what education's all about – assessing a student's potential and performance, and helping him or her to reach high standards of achievement.'

**C** **Emma Rees-Baker** is a secondary school teacher, so she knows what she's talking about. 'It seems to me we should be looking for talent in everybody, trying to discover what that person is about, helping them to develop as a creative, thinking individual. So in my classes (I teach art), we do spend some time on theory, but practical work is far more important. And that means that tests and exams have to be practically based too. Actually I believe pupils studying *any* subject learn best by doing practical tasks, but I suppose it's easier to see the point with art. I mean, you wouldn't be much good as an artist if you knew the theory off by heart but couldn't produce a painting, would you?! But don't think all this means there's chaos in my classroom. I also believe teachers must maintain control at all times.'

**D** **Robert Wagstaff** has been studying computer engineering at university for the last two years. He says the media give the wrong impression of student life. 'It's not that easy being a student. Older people often seem to think we're living in the lap of luxury, all at the expense of the taxpayer! Well, I can tell you, nothing could be further from the truth. Most students I know live in pretty bad conditions, and have difficulty managing their money. And most of us study really hard, sometimes all night. You have to, to be able to hand in your projects and assignments on time. Otherwise you get thrown out of university. So you need to discipline yourself, which is a lot more difficult than someone telling you what to do. Occasionally I ask myself why I'm doing it, but I know the reason. I want a really good job – well, that's the point of all this studying, isn't it?'

**E** Finally, retired teacher **Geraldine Bickerton** has something to say. 'It's very important to have a good education. And by that I mean being taught 'the three R's', as we used to say – Reading, Writing and Arithmetic – when you're young. And children should learn proper respect for their elders and betters, especially in the classroom. Far too many young people simply don't understand that they'll never get anywhere if they don't study and learn things. Life these days is getting more and more complicated – I mean, I can't record a programme on my video without my granddaughter's help – and if people haven't had a decent education, they just won't be able to cope. Youngsters today are so lucky – they have all these schools and colleges to choose from. They should make the most of it. *My* generation never had the choice.'

You are going to read an extract from the novel *Sour Sweet* by Timothy Mo, about a Chinese family living in the UK. For questions 1 – 8, choose the most appropriate answer (A, B, C or D) to each question.

The Chens had been living in the UK for four years, which was long enough to have lost their place in the society from which they had emigrated but not long enough to feel comfortable in the new. They
5 were no longer missed; Lily had no living relatives anyway, apart from her sister Mui, and Chen had lost his claim to clan land in his ancestral village. He was remembered there in the shape of the money order he remitted to his father every month, and would
10 truly have been remembered only if that order failed to arrive.

But in the UK, land of promise, Chen was still an interloper. He regarded himself as such. True, he paid reasonable rent to Brent Council for warm and
15 comfortable accommodation, quarters which were positively palatial compared to those which his wife Lily had known in Hong Kong. That English people had competed for the flat which he now occupied made Chen feel more rather than less of a foreigner;
20 it made him feel like a gatecrasher who had stayed too long and been identified. He had no tangible reason to feel like this. No one had yet so much as looked twice at him. But Chen knew, felt it in his bones, could sense it between his shoulder-
25 blades as he walked past emptying public houses on his day off; in an unspoken complicity between himself and others like him, not necessarily of his race. A huge West Indian bus conductor regularly undercharged him on his morning journey to work.
30 He knew because the English one charged him threepence more. Chen was sure the black man's mistake was deliberate. He put the threepences for luck in an outgrown sock of his little son, Man Kee. Chen was not an especially superstitious man but
35 there were times, he felt, when you needed all the luck you could lay your hands on.

Chen's week had a certain stark simplicity about it. He worked seventy-two hours at his restaurant, slept fifty-six, spent forty hours with his wife and
40 child (more like thirty-two minus travelling time, and, of course, Man Kee was often asleep when he was awake). This was on a rotation of six days a week at the restaurant with one off (Thursday). That day was spent in recuperation on his back on the sofa, generally with open eyes, for his feet ached after the 45 hours of standing. It was hard and the money came at a cost but he wasn't complaining: the wages were spectacularly good, even forgetting the tips.

Lily Chen always prepared an 'evening' snack for her husband to consume on his return at 1.15 a.m. 50 This was not strictly necessary since Chen enjoyed at the unusually late hour of 11.45 p.m. what the boss boasted was the best employees' dinner in any restaurant. They sat, waiters, boss, boss's mother too, at a round table and ate soup, a huge 55 fish, vegetables, shredded pork, and a tureen of steaming rice. Lily still went ahead and prepared broth, golden-yellow with floating oily rings, and put it before her husband when he returned. She felt she would have been failing in her wifely duties 60 otherwise. Dutifully, Chen drank the soup he raised to his mouth in the patterned porcelain spoon while Lily watched him closely from the sofa. It was far too rich for him. Four years ago, at the beginning of their marriage, Chen had tried leaving just the last 65 spoonful but Lily's reproachful eyes were intolerable. She was merciless now, watching him with sidelong glances from the sofa, her knees pressed closely together while she paired the baby's socks from the plastic basket on the floor. 'Did you enjoy that, 70 Husband? Was it nice?' she would enquire brightly. Chen would grunt in his stolid way, not wishing to hurt her feelings but also careful not to let himself in for a bigger bowl in the future.

Although uncomfortably full, hot too, Chen would 75 have liked a biscuit but Lily was unrelenting here as well. Sweet after salty was dangerous for the system, so she had been taught; it could upset the whole balance of the dualistic or female and male principles, *yin* and *yang*. For four years, therefore, 80 Chen had been going to bed tortured with the last extremities of thirst but with his dualistic male and female principles in harmony. This was more than could be said for Lily, Chen often thought, who concealed a steely will behind her demure exterior. 85

1  In the first paragraph, what was the attitude of Chen's relatives towards him?

   **A**  They were proud of his achievements.

   **B**  They remembered him with affection.

   **C**  They valued him for his financial support.

   **D**  They wanted him to return to farm his land.

2  The writer uses the expression 'land of promise' in line 12 to suggest

   **A**  how well Chen has done in his new surroundings.

   **B**  Chen's commitment to the UK.

   **C**  what Chen was guaranteed before he emigrated.

   **D**  the contrast between Chen's expectations and the reality.

3  How did Chen feel about living in the UK?

   **A**  nervous about looking different

   **B**  relieved that he was beginning to fit in

   **C**  sorry for English people who had nowhere to live

   **D**  disappointed that no one noticed him

4  According to Chen, the bus conductor undercharged him because

   **A**  they both believed in luck.

   **B**  it gave them something to talk about.

   **C**  they both felt like foreigners.

   **D**  the fares were difficult to calculate.

5  What was Chen's opinion of his job?

   **A**  He was physically unsuited to it.

   **B**  Its advantages outweighed its disadvantages.

   **C**  He urgently needed a pay rise.

   **D**  Its predictability was its best feature.

6  Lily prepared a snack for her husband because

   **A**  he expected it.

   **B**  she thought he would be hungry.

   **C**  she considered she ought to.

   **D**  he preferred eating at home.

7  What do we learn about the relationship between Chen and Lily?

   **A**  He did not want to upset her.

   **B**  He found it difficult to understand her.

   **C**  She enjoyed watching him suffer.

   **D**  She was forced to accept his beliefs.

8  What does 'This was more than could be said for Lily' in lines 83 – 4 refer to?

   **A**  She never complained of thirst.

   **B**  She hid many things from her husband.

   **C**  Her theories about food were unusual.

   **D**  Her male and female elements were not in harmony.

# Part 2

You are going to read a newspaper article about a sailor called Tristan Jones. Seven sentences have been removed from the article. Choose from the sentences A – H the one which fits each gap. There is one extra sentence.

## AMAZING LIFE OF THE OLD MAN OF THE SEA

One of the great seafaring eccentrics, Tristan Jones, died in 1995 at the age of 71. Like Long John Silver, he had lost a leg – though in his case the replacement was made of plastic.
5 | 9 | He never had much money, recognition or fame, but he has been called the greatest lone sailor of our age.

Tristan Jones was born at sea, on his father's ship as it rounded Cape Horn. Though brought
10 up in Wales, he spent most of his life sailing boats single-handedly, and went four times round the world. He claimed to have sailed 400,000 miles, mostly alone, and held dozens of records.

15 He went to sea when he was fourteen and was sunk three times before his nineteenth birthday. During the war he served as a stoker* on the battleship Warspite, rising to petty officer three times, but each time being
20 demoted to stoker – 'for fighting,' he said. | 10 | For most, that would have been the end of a seafaring career. For Tristan Jones, it was the start of his solo sailing.

| 11 | His craft was an antique lifeboat
25 powered by an old London Fire Brigade pumping engine. For a year and a day he was trapped in the ice, yet he got within 285 miles of the record. The voyage took two years and the book he wrote about it, *Ice*, is a classic.

30 The Arctic voyage, funded by his £3-a-week Navy pension, was only the beginning. Afterwards, desperate for money, he went back to stoking boilers – this time in Harrods*,

where he lived off scraps from the food hall.
| 12 | 35

Jones's last round-the-world voyage was from west to east – the hard way. He said the sunsets looked so much better when seen from the stern*. As well as going round the world, he held the record for the greatest vertical voyage 40 – from the Dead Sea in Israel, 1,310 feet below sea level, to Lake Titicaca in the Peruvian Andes, the world's highest lake at 12,505 feet. | 13 | The book he wrote about those three weeks of hell in the jungle – *The Incredible* 45 *Voyage* – became another bestseller.

Frequently his journeys were halted by poverty: he would hole up in a port, write another book, and on the proceeds sail on. Altogether he wrote seventeen marine 50 adventure stories, two novels and dozens of short stories.

Part of his last round-the-world epic included a journey overland. | 14 | With a group of three disabled Thai youths, he sailed as far up 55 the Trang River as he could. Then he enlisted an Indian elephant and the Thai army to drag the boat nine miles to the headwaters of the Tapee river.

| 15 | 'Why do you do it?' they asked. 60 His answer: 'You get up one day and think you would like to go to New Guinea. So you go.'

Tristan Jones said once: 'I've sailed an ocean-going craft as close to heaven as may be done until man finds water among the stars.' As an 65 epitaph for a sailor, it will serve.

*stoker: person whose job is to put fuel in a boiler
*Harrods: famous department store in London

*stern: back end of a boat

**A** With Nelson, he ventured into the Arctic, trying to beat the record for the farthest north any boat had got.

**B** His sole crew on his many voyages was Nelson, a three-legged, one-eyed labrador he inherited when the captain of his first sailing boat died.

**C** 'I like being my own boss – sailing's the only work I've ever done,' he used to say.

**D** People found his exploits thrilling but some never understood what motivated him.

**E** From there he sailed up the Amazon and, starving, hacked his way through the dense swamps of the Mato Grosso in Brazil.

**F** He was sailing the 28-foot Henry Wagner to the South China Sea from the Indian Ocean, and the Kra Isthmus that joins Malaysia to Singapore was in the way.

**G** Disabled out of the Navy when guerrillas blew up his ship in Aden, he was told he would never walk again.

**H** As soon as he had saved enough for a boat, he was off again.

# Part 3

You are going to read part of a magazine article on health. For questions 16 – 30, choose from the people (A – E). The people may be chosen more than once.

**Who implies or states the following opinions?**

The national health service cannot always provide the most up-to-date care. ☐ 16

It is the government's responsibility to provide comprehensive healthcare. ☐ 17

Doctors have difficulty in meeting all the demands of their patients. ☐ 18

Individuals will need to take out insurance to cover unexpected health problems. ☐ 19

Orthodox medicine is not always the best way to treat illness. ☐ 20

A healthy lifestyle means that you rarely need medical help. ☐ 21 ☐ 22

Healthcare provision is deteriorating. ☐ 23 ☐ 24

There is more mental illness these days, as a result of the pressures of modern life. ☐ 25

Waiting lists for pain-relieving operations are unacceptable. ☐ 26

It is an employer's duty to provide a safe and healthy working environment. ☐ 27

It is important to look at the whole person when trying to treat a patient, not just the symptoms. ☐ 28

Scientific research has not been able to solve all medical problems. ☐ 29 ☐ 30

# GOOD HEALTH FOR ALL

**Most people have strong views on what makes or keeps them healthy, as well as what kind of healthcare they expect.**

**A** **Dr Andrew Page** is a family doctor, with about two thousand patients in his care. He finds it a rewarding but stressful job. 'We do our best, but sometimes that doesn't seem to be enough. Patients often expect the impossible. I've lost count of the times I've been called out in the middle of the night for very trivial reasons, but even if it's just a sore throat that's ruined my night's sleep, I still have to be courteous and professional. And patients assume we can cure them, but medicine is still evolving – we haven't got all the answers yet. What people should really try to do is eat properly, take exercise and stay fit – you know the old saying, an apple a day keeps the doctor away. Then we wouldn't have such long queues in our waiting rooms.'

**B** **Josephine Cartland** is 76, and has had her name down for a hip replacement operation for six months. She is in constant pain from arthritis. Recently the hospital informed her that she is still near the bottom of the list. She is furious. 'Why should I have to hang on like this? My husband and I have paid our taxes all our lives. I think it's up to the state to make sure we get doctors, medicines and operations when we need them, whatever's wrong with us. And we shouldn't have to pay either! Do they realise what pain I'm in? I don't think they care! Things are getting worse and worse with the health service.'

**C** **Francesca Lewis**, 25, is a dancer with an international ballet company. 'I must admit I hardly ever go to the doctor. I suppose it's because I really have to take care of myself in my job. We exercise a lot, obviously, and I'm very careful what I eat. I avoid processed foods, I never drink or smoke, and I don't have late nights. Rather boring, but very healthy! And if I ever get ill, I don't do much about it. If it's flu, I might stay in bed for a couple of days, but if it's just a cold, I usually pay no attention – just carry on with my normal routine. I can guarantee it works!'

**D** **Tony Baines** is a trained acupuncturist who has had years of experience treating all sorts of problems. He is also a qualified doctor, and this enables him to compare the two systems of oriental and western medicine. He is convinced that alternative therapies, such as acupuncture and homeopathy, often bring much greater benefits to the patient than the more traditional treatments prescribed by the family doctor. 'For one thing, we don't limit ourselves to examining the patient's symptoms. Our holistic approach means we consider diet, weight, previous illnesses, allergies, worries, lifestyle, everything, before we make a diagnosis.'

**E** **Carol Nicholson** is a hospital manager, whose main aim is to provide the right care for patients while keeping within a tight budget. 'Medical care has become so expensive these days that government funding is just not sufficient any more. Hospitals can no longer guarantee total healthcare for everyone. There comes a point where the state simply cannot meet the bills, especially for some of the more complex treatments that have been developed in recent years. In future, people will have to be prepared to cover themselves against sudden or extended illness – the premiums are not unreasonable.'

She points out that current lifestyles often contribute to or cause health problems. 'For example, we see a lot of work-related cases in the Accident and Emergency Department, although there is a legal obligation on companies to protect their employees. Another area of concern is that of the psychiatric ill-health suffered by a cross-section of society, because of the stress they encounter these days. The solutions to these problems, whether social or medical, have not yet been found, despite the best efforts of our scientists.'

You are going to read part of a magazine article about a reporter, Sue Lloyd-Roberts. For questions 1 – 8, choose the most appropriate answer (A, B, C or D) to each question.

My work as a BBC TV foreign correspondent means that I spend about one week in five abroad. I specialise in human rights and environmental stories and travel alone, as a one-woman crew. But when I'm not abroad, I'm at home in North London, with my two children.

5  I'm often asked why I do such a crazy job when I've got children, but in actual fact I'm outside the school gates far more often than a high-powered woman who's, say, an MP or a company executive, because I can dictate my own schedules. I don't do sudden news stories and choose never to go into war zones, so the danger is minimal.

10  Working alone as both reporter and cameraman suits me perfectly because I do very little eating and sleeping on trips and I don't think a crew would appreciate having to fit in with me. I also cut down the amount of time I'm away from home by using the nights to travel. In Iraq once, I slept through two nine-hour car journeys across the desert, so I could hit the ground running
15  when I arrived.

At home, my day begins with BBC1's Breakfast News at 7 a.m. If I'm in it, the children sit on the end of my bed and watch it with me, although they're usually more concerned about where their breakfast is. When they've gone to school, I do thirty lengths of the local pool – my only keep-fit activity – before starting
20  work. I'm always planning several future trips and have lunch with various opposition leaders, former diplomats and their fellow workers three or four times a week. London is a very good place to establish these contacts.

The day before I travel is always an at-home day, for packing, checking my equipment and spending time with the children. I have to clean my camera
25  – a top-of-the range Sony UXI – and make sure I've got all the necessary videotapes, lenses, bulbs and batteries. I travel so lightly that I could easily be mistaken for a tourist, although if I'm in a country where they're likely to be a bit suspicious, I leave my tripod behind. I'm sure that it helps to be a woman because whenever I'm questioned by the authorities, I play the middle-aged
30  housewife and they usually let me go.

I'm not a domesticated animal so our nanny, Julie, usually cooks the evening meal. But on a pre-travel day I give her the evening off so we can be alone as a family. I'm sure it's sometimes difficult for the kids, but there is a plus side as they're quite involved in what I do and have met all sorts of interesting people
35  at our house. My daughter has the best foreign doll collection in London! But I'm prepared for the possibility that one day they'll turn round and say, 'Where were you, Mum?'

**1** Which of the following statements is true?

   **A** Most of Sue's time is spent working abroad.

   **B** She travels with only one cameraman.

   **C** When at home in London, she devotes all her time to the children.

   **D** She concentrates on particular issues in her reports.

**2** What does she think about her career and motherhood?

   **A** It's madness trying to be a mother *and* a foreign correspondent.

   **B** Her timetable is flexible so she can be available for her children.

   **C** Having children gives her insight into situations of conflict.

   **D** She would really prefer to be a high-powered camerawoman.

**3** How has she adapted physically to her job?

   **A** She needs very little food or sleep.

   **B** She sleeps while travelling in order to save money.

   **C** She needs exercise when she arrives in a new place.

   **D** She is psychologically unsuited to working in a team.

**4** How does she spend her day at home?

   **A** She gets involved in various sporting activities.

   **B** She often has lunch with members of the government.

   **C** She spends a lot of time getting information for future projects.

   **D** The first thing is to get breakfast for the children.

**5** How does being a woman help her in her job?

   **A** She is able to check and clean all her equipment herself.

   **B** She may not be recognised as a reporter.

   **C** She only needs light clothing.

   **D** She can sometimes manage without her tripod.

**6** What arrangements for childcare has she made?

   **A** Her parents regularly collect the children from school.

   **B** She pays a babysitter to cook supper every day.

   **C** She takes sole responsibility for childcare all the time she is at home.

   **D** She has a nanny who comes whenever necessary.

**7** What are the effects of her job on her children?

   **A** They are gaining an awareness of the issues she specialises in.

   **B** They often complain about her absences.

   **C** They both have an excellent collection of souvenirs.

   **D** They can sometimes be difficult to cope with.

**8** How do you think she feels about her job?

   **A** worried about losing it

   **B** optimistic about changing it later

   **C** enthusiastic about doing it

   **D** fed up with the problems it involves

# Part 2

You are going to read part of an article about modern working conditions. Seven sentences have been removed from the article. Choose from the sentences A – H the one which fits each gap. There is one extra sentence.

## WORK TILL YOU DROP

**9 [        ]** I can see a jumbled montage of postcards on a pinboard, a gaunt plant with crinkled leaves and a faint glimmer of daylight between drawn blinds. **10 [        ]** All around there is an anarchic mess of documents, as if I have stumbled into a refugee camp for paperwork: books piled high,
5   notebooks filled and flung to one side, magazines half read and covered in a fine layer of dust. The room flickers in a the glow of a fluorescent light.

Air conditioning hums in the background. Telephones screech. A colleague is shouting down the phone. **11 [        ]** A third chatters to herself as she writes, like an excited songbird.

10  It is just another day in *The Guardian*'s Farringdon Road offices, and I'm feeling anything but fine. My nose is doing a double act: one nostril blocked, the other pouring. My back aches, leg muscles are atrophying* from disuse, and my brain feels like it has been cling-wrapped in sandpaper.

**12 [        ]** After you have scrambled into the office today and slumped
15  breathless into a chair, sit back. Look around. Savour the air. Listen to the cacophany*. If you still feel happy, you are lucky. The physical world of work, it seems, is eroding the strength of many of us.

The Health and Safety Executive has brought out a report that aims to spread the message that offices can seriously damage your health.
20  **13 [        ]** The HSE says that an edifice can be diagnosed 'sick' where staff complain of being ill more commonly than might be reasonably expected. **14 [        ]** Seven out of ten office workers reported symptoms at work such as runny noses, tight chests and lethargy* – symptoms that vanished the instant they quit the building. **15 [        ]** Elements at work
25  such as dodgy* air conditioning, low humidity, and excessive heat and dust, can act as a sort of poison, making employees tired and worn out, irritating their eyes, noses and throats, and constricting breath.

*atrophying:* losing strength, wasting away          *lethargy:* lack of energy
*cacophony:* noise                                    *dodgy:* defective

**A** Company auditors complain that overheads are rising, due to increased energy costs.

**B** Another thumps his keyboard as a child bashes a piano.

**C** In an attempt to explain these grumblings, academics have come up with the notion that aspects of the building itself are to blame.

**D** Just how frequent such complaints have become is highlighted in a joint study by architecture schools in Cardiff and London.

**E** If you think that sounds bad, pause and reflect on your own working conditions.

**F** I am sitting in a room with a view.

**G** Following terminology coined in the United States, it calls the malaise Sick Building Syndrome.

**H** Banks of desks, screens, faxes and photocopiers stretch into the distance.

# Part 3

You are going to read part of an article about London. For questions 16 – 30, choose from the sections (A – E). The sections may be chosen more than once.

**Which section mentions**

a dress code? | 16 |

a comparison with a European state? | 17 |

appealingly authentic places to eat and drink? | 18 |

a tip for economising on visits to shows? | 19 |

a form of transport suitable for tourists? | 20 |

the difficulty of deciding what to go and see? | 21 |

places which have been popular with tourists for a long time? | 22 |

a simple way of finding information? | 23 |

the impression of being in a rural environment? | 24 |

a sense of rivalry? | 25 |

evening venues which are currently fashionable? | 26 |

advice on how to choose accommodation? | 27 |

a historical aspect to some dramatic performances? | 28 |

why shoppers are attracted to London? | 29 |

the importance of maintaining an image? | 30 |

# LONDON IN WINTER

**A** THERE'S NOTHING NICER on a fine winter's afternoon than to take a brisk country walk. But did you know you can do this in London? The city's favourite 'country' walk takes you more or less in a straight line across the former royal hunting grounds of Kensington Gardens, Hyde Park, Green Park and St James's Park. These vast open spaces dotted with gleaming lakes sprawl across central London like a great green carpet and you only cross a couple of main roads during the entire walk.

The sheer size of this city-centre playground doesn't really register until you walk across it. There are entire countries smaller than this! Kensington Gardens and Hyde Park together cover some 600 acres – an area larger than the principality of Monaco.

The River Thames can look especially beautiful in winter and there are countless attractions lining its banks. Or you can catch a riverboat from Charing Cross Pier, either upstream to Hampton Court Palace or downstream to Greenwich, home of the famous Royal Observatory.

→

**B** THE NATION'S CAPITAL doesn't close down just because it is winter, any more than it closes down after dark. After all, it has got a reputation to live up to: that of being one of the most exciting cities in the world. In December, the Christmas lights turn Oxford Street and Regent Street into a glittering fairyland and the big stores compete with one another to see which of them can produce the most magical window display.

The biggest shopping centre in the world is right here, in the heart of London – in the area bounded by Oxford Street, Regent Street, Bond Street and Piccadilly. Whatever you want to buy, you can find it in this huge, golden rectangle. And, come the January sales, you can buy it more cheaply too.

The sales have become an institution – and a massive tourist attraction. The big stores have become such an important part of the London shopping scene that they can afford to make their own rules. Harrods won't let you into the store if you are wearing cut-off shorts or a vest, or if you are carrying a rucksack.

If you are visiting London and want to know what to buy and where, including details about the January sales, then you will get all the help you need by accessing www.londontown.com or www.visitlondon.com.

**C** ANOTHER TRADITIONAL ACTIVITY IN LONDON besides shopping is theatre-going. The range of shows covers everything from top musicals to plays by Shakespeare. The latter are more interesting now that the Elizabethan-style Globe Theatre has opened at Bankside. And, of course, over Christmas and New Year, the pantomime season is in full swing.

For tickets to West End shows, try the half-price booth in Leicester Square: it opens at 10 a.m. to sell tickets for that evening's performances. Alternatively, the Tourist Information Centres at Victoria Station, Liverpool Street Station and Heathrow all sell theatre tickets, although they charge full price. Add the jazz at Ronnie Scott's in Soho and a few other nightspots (Moonlighting and Hanover Grand are 'in' places), and that's your after-dark entertainment looked after.

**D** LONDON'S MUSEUMS are at the top of many visitors' lists. Lesser-known ones include Sir John Soane's unique and extraordinary collection of art and antiquities at 13 Lincoln's Inn Fields, Florence Nightingale's Museum at St Thomas' Hospital, and the fascinating Bank of England Museum. But don't miss old favourites such as the Natural History Museum, the Science Museum, the Victoria and Albert Museum, and, last but not least, the world-famous British Museum.

**E** IF YOU ARE NOT A REGULAR VISITOR to London, the choice of things to do can be bewildering. So can the selection of restaurants and the number of places to stay. The important rule is, don't be guided by price. When it comes to eating and sleeping, price is not always an indication of quality.

After a hard day's shopping or sightseeing you might want to relax in the unique atmosphere of Ye Olde Cheshire Cheese pub in Fleet Street, already well known in the 17th century, or enjoy an entrecôte steak with herb-butter sauce, the speciality of Rowley's in Jermyn Street. You can find plastic pubs and hamburger joints anywhere, but these are the real thing.

# Part 1

You are going to read an extract from *As I Walked Out One Midsummer Morning* by Laurie Lee. For questions 1 – 8, choose the most appropriate answer (A, B, C or D) to each question.

The stooping figure of my mother, waist-deep in the grass and caught there like a piece of sheep's wool, was the last I saw of my country home as I left it to discover the world. She stood old and bent at the top of the bank, silently watching me go, one gnarled red hand raised in farewell and
5   blessing, not questioning why I went. At the bend of the road I looked back again and saw the gold light die behind her; then I turned the corner, passed the village school, and closed that part of my life forever.

It was a bright Sunday morning in early June, the right time to be leaving home. My three sisters and a brother had already gone before me; two
10  other brothers had yet to make up their minds. They were still sleeping that morning, but my mother had got up early and cooked me a heavy breakfast, had stood wordlessly while I ate it, her hand on my chair, and had then helped me pack up my few belongings. There had been no fuss, no appeals, no attempts at advice or persuasion, only a long and searching look. Then,
15  with my bags on my back, I'd gone out into the early sunshine and climbed through the long wet grass to the road.

It was 1934. I was nineteen years old, still soft at the edges, but with a confident belief in good fortune. I carried a small rolled-up tent, a violin in a blanket, a change of clothes, a tin of treacle biscuits and some cheese. I
20  was excited, knowing I had far to go; but not, as yet, how far. As I left home that morning and walked away from the sleeping village, it never occurred to me that others had done this before me.

I was propelled, of course, by the traditional forces that had sent many generations along this road – by the small tight valley closing in around me,
25  stifling the breath with its mossy mouth, the cottage walls narrowing, the local girls whispering, 'Marry, and settle down.'

And now I was on my journey, in a pair of thick boots and with a stick in my hand. Naturally, I was going to London, which lay a hundred miles to the east; and it seemed equally obvious that I should go on foot. But
30  first, as I'd never yet seen the sea, I thought I'd walk to the coast and find it. This would add another hundred miles to my journey, going by way of Southampton. But I had all the summer and all time to spend.

As I tramped through the dust towards the Wiltshire Downs a growing reluctance weighed me down. Through the solitary morning and afternoon
35  I found myself longing for some opposition or rescue, for the sound of hurrying footsteps coming after me and family voices calling me back.

None came. I was free. The day's silence said, Go where you will. It's all yours. You asked for it. It's up to you now. You're on your own and nobody's going to stop you.

**1** In the first paragraph, what does the writer stress when describing his mother?

   **A** her age

   **B** her anger

   **C** her lack of importance in his life

   **D** her inability to leave the village

**2** On the day the writer left home, his mother

   **A** encouraged him to leave.

   **B** advised him the best time to leave.

   **C** asked him why he was leaving.

   **D** accepted his decision to leave.

**3** How did the writer feel as he started out?

   **A** sure that he could manage on his own

   **B** curious about others who had left home

   **C** sad at leaving his childhood environment

   **D** worried about the distance he would have to travel

**4** What was the writer's reason for leaving home?

   **A** His girlfriend had asked him to marry her.

   **B** He wanted to live in a more spacious house.

   **C** He was keen to broaden his experience.

   **D** It was a family tradition to move out at nineteen.

**5** In the paragraph beginning on line 27, the writer suggests that his journey

   **A** had been carefully planned.

   **B** would achieve a particular ambition of his.

   **C** would only be partly done on foot.

   **D** had to be completed by the end of the summer.

**6** The writer says that, while on his way to the Wiltshire Downs, he

   **A** felt unwilling to return.

   **B** began to regret leaving home.

   **C** became excited at the thought of his adventure.

   **D** enjoyed the feeling of having no responsibilities.

**7** The writer refers to 'the day's silence' in line 37 in order to show

   **A** his own selfishness.

   **B** his liking for peace and quiet.

   **C** his awareness of being alone.

   **D** his family's lack of affection for him.

**8** What does 'it' in 'you asked for it' (line 38) refer to?

   **A** the countryside

   **B** the day

   **C** his destination

   **D** his freedom

# Part 2

You are going to read part of an article about the city of Venice. Seven sentences have been removed from the article. Choose from the sentences A – H the one which fits each gap. There is one extra sentence.

## THE REAL VENICE

To begin with, Venice is small. The sweep of the vistas across the Venetian Lagoon, the immense, moody arc of the sky, the grandiose facades – all give the illusion of amplitude*. So it comes as a shock to learn that Venice, with its 150 canals, 409 bridges, 3,000 alleyways and 117 islands, covers a mere three square miles. **9** And you will walk, because the streets are usually the size of an average pavement. Walking, as much as the surrounding water, dictates the shape of Venetian life: the reasonable pace, the sudden street-corner encounters with friends, the pause to talk. **10** They like to say their city is like a living room.

Is Venice still sinking? **11** In a word, yes, though the rate has slowed, mainly because the pumping of groundwater for industries on the mainland has been stopped. Flooding occurs regularly between November and March. The catastrophic flood of November 4, 1966 inundated parts of the city with as much as four feet of water for twenty-four hours. The ground floors of some 16,000 houses were abandoned altogether. **12**

But today a rising tide of troubles is more likely to swamp the city. A new sense of desperation seems to have taken hold. **13** As many as 1,500 people a year leave Venice, especially young families unwilling to cope with the cost of living and finding a good job and an affordable house or apartment. **14** The situation has become so bad that depopulation is reaching the point of no return. Venice may become a city of virtually no residents within the next 30 years, turning into a sort of Italian Disneyland, teeming with tourists but empty of inhabitants.

Yet Venetians love their city, and most have known one another from birth. They are also essentially island people, living offshore in their own self-contained universe. **15** She is a senior assistant at a museum; her Venetian parents moved to the mainland, but she moved back. 'Every time I leave Venice, I have not only psychological pain but physical pain too. Deep pain. It's stupid; I can't explain it. When you're away, you feel that something is lost. Because here people are different, relationships are different, houses are different, *everything* is different. When I see the lagoon from the plane, I thank God that I'm back.'

*amplitude: large size

**A** Since then, a tremendous international effort has been made to repair the palaces and churches, restore the works of art and protect the surrounding lagoon from future tidal calamity.

**B** Among the many things the Venetians love about their city – no cars, virtually no violent crime – this intimacy is the best.

**C** 'I don't like going to the mainland,' one elderly gondolier told me, 'and I only ever go by boat.'

**D** These are the unglamorous facts of life in any city.

**E** You could stroll from one end to the other in an hour.

**F** 'Venice is a place that overwhelms you,' Clarenza Catullo said frankly as we sat at dinner one winter evening.

**G** This is the question everybody outside Venice seems to ask.

**H** Businesses have moved out; the population has halved over the past fifty years to a mere 62,000.

# Part 3

You are going to read part of a guidebook entry on New Zealand's North Island. For questions 16 – 30, choose from the sections (A – E). The sections may be chosen more than once.

**Which section mentions**

an area full of interesting geological features? [16] [    ]

some of the risks involved in a particular activity? [17] [    ]

an activity likely to be recommended by a doctor? [18] [    ]

an exception to a strict rule? [19] [    ]

the use of special lighting to change creatures' habits? [20] [    ]

a town surrounded by mountains? [21] [    ]

exhibits of international origin? [22] [    ]

areas with historical connections from different periods? [23] [    ]

several long-established tourist attractions? [24] [    ]

restricted access which can be overcome? [25] [    ]

a special area for young children? [26] [    ]

a wide range of sporting options? [27] [    ]

an impressive object once used for military purposes? [28] [    ]

the reason why a place gained its reputation? [29] [    ]

people's efforts to achieve a change in policy? [30] [    ]

## A Auckland and Waipoua

If you're only going to see one thing in Auckland, see one of the city's magnificent museums. The Auckland Museum has a tremendous display of Maori artefacts and culture: pride of place goes to a magnificent 25-metre-long war canoe, but there are many other examples of the Maoris' arts and lifestyle. The museum also houses a fine display of South Pacific items and New Zealand wildlife, and displays thousands of other interesting objects from around the world.

The road north enters the Waipoua Kauri Forest 50 km out of Dargaville. The Waipoua Kauri Forest Sanctuary, proclaimed in 1952 after much public pressure, is the largest remnant of the once extensive kauri forests of northern New Zealand. There is no cutting of mature kauri trees nowadays, except under extraordinary circumstances such as the carving of a Maori canoe.

The road through the forest passes by some splendid huge kauris. Turn off to the forest lookout just after you enter the park – it was once a fire lookout and offers spectacular views.

## B Otorohanga and Waitomo

The well-signposted Otorohanga Kiwi House is the town's main attraction and worth a visit. In a kiwi house night and day are reversed, so you can watch the birds in daytime under artificial moonlight. The walk-in aviary is the largest in New Zealand and houses various other native birds. The Kiwi House is open from 9 am to 4.30 pm every day, except from June to August when it closes at 4 pm.

Waitomo (population 300) is famous for its limestone caves; the whole region is riddled with caves and strange limestone formations. Tours through the Waitomo Caves (also called the Glowworm Caves), the Ruakuri Cave and the Aranui Cave have been feature attractions for decades.

In recent years a whole new batch of activities has cropped up – organised caving expeditions, rafting through caves, abseiling and various combinations of the three, plus horse trekking, white water rafting and more.

## C Mount Taranaki

Due to its easy accessibility, Mt Taranaki ranks as the 'most climbed' mountain in New Zealand. Nevertheless, hiking on this mountain holds definite dangers and should not be undertaken lightly. The principal hazard is the erratic weather, which can change from warm, sunny 'shorts weather' to raging gales and white-out conditions amazingly quickly and unexpectedly; snow can come at any time of year on the mountain, even in summer. In good conditions, hiking around the mountain, or even to the summit, can be reasonably easy, but the mountain has claimed over 50 lives. Don't be put off, but don't be deceived.

## D Thames and Whitianga

The town of Thames is known as the 'Gateway to the Coromandel Peninsula' and is the region's main commercial centre, boasting a wealth of boutique-style shops. In the late 19th century Thames was one of New Zealand's largest towns, built on the pioneering industries of gold and kauri logging. It was even considered as a site for the capital. Fringing the town are the dramatic volcanic hills of the Coromandel range and Kauaeranga Valley.

The pleasant Whitianga area of Mercury Bay has a long history, by New Zealand standards. The Polynesian explorer Kupe landed near here around 950 AD. Mercury Bay was given its modern name by Captain Cook when he observed the transit of the planet Mercury while anchored in the bay in November 1769. The town is a big-game fishing base for tuna, marlin, mako, thresher shark and kingfish.

→

### E  Lake Taupo and Waikite

The Lake Taupo region is home to New Zealand's largest freshwater lake. Three
95 boats specialise in cruises on the lake: the *Barbary*, the *Spirit of Musick* and the *Ernest Kemp.* All three boats offer similar trips, visiting a modern Maori rock carving beside the lake. The carving is on private
100 land so it cannot be reached on foot; the only way to see it is by boat. The cruises last about 2½ to 3 hours.

Waikite Valley Thermal Pools is a unique place to go to experience the beneficial mineral waters of the Te Manaroa Spring. 105 The naturally warm waters cascade into the main splash pool (35 – 38°C), the adjoining toddlers' beach area, and the luxurious new Tranquil Garden pool. Situated in a rural area 25 minutes south 110 of Rotorua off SH5, Waikite Thermal Valley is the perfect place to relax and unwind all year round.

*Mount Taranaki*

# Key

## Section 1

## Unit 1

A The writer is describing his/her daily journey to school.

B It is important to choose the right kind of holiday.

C An old woman is comparing her past with her present.

D Traditional ways of farming in Spain are being lost because of (the impact of ) tourism.

E There have been cuts in water supplies because of recent drought/very dry conditions in Europe, so people and water companies are now more interested in saving water.

F The city authorities are introducing a number of measures in order to reduce air pollution.

G Research in New Zealand shows that hidden cameras, rather than highly visible ones, may be the best way to slow down traffic over a wide area.

H Children who get several mild infections early in life are less likely to develop allergies later. / Parents should not try to keep their children completely free from dirt or bacteria.

I There are various ways in which people who suffer from insomnia can improve their sleep patterns.

## Unit 2

A 1C  2A  3B  4B/D  5E  6B/C  7C  8G  9F  10B

B  1 Camp Beaumont
   2 Canadian Affair
   3 Chinese State Circus, Preston Park, Brighton
   4 Annual Festival of Scottish Dance, Wyeside Arts Centre, Hereford
   5 Rough Magic
   6 Festival of English Food and Wine, Leeds Castle, Maidstone
   7 Hoseasons
   8 David Austin
   9 Farmer, 40
   10 Adams Antiques Fair, Royal Horticultural Society Halls, London

C 1C  2E  3H  4J  5G  6A  7B  8D  9A  10F  11I

D 1F  2A  3H  4G  5C  6D  7E

## Practice 1

A  1 Britain
   2 mental illness / hereditary blood disorder
   3 1795: Prince George and Princess Caroline got married. 1820: George III died and his son George became King George IV.
   4 George III, father of George IV. George IV was married to Princess Caroline. They had a daughter, Princess Charlotte.
   5 Westminster Abbey
   6 He was delighted.
   7 He hoped Parliament would pay his bills and give him more money.
   8 He did not like her.
   9 Charlotte
   10 to be crowned queen
   11 immoral behaviour
   12 She had no ticket for the coronation.

B  1 Humans and animals may be allergic to it.
   2 the processionary caterpillar
   3 about 600,000
   4 a big fluffy white ball

5   at the top of pine trees
6   cats and dogs
7   They might be seriously hurt or die.
8   call a vet at once
9   the local authorities

C   1   a large round table, once believed to be King Arthur's Round Table
2   no
3   between the railway station and the river
4   11th century
5   Jane Austen
6   They wear red badges.
7   during services / starting at 8 am and 5.30 pm
8   20th century

# Unit 3

A   1   a) shanty towns   b) litter   c) voluntary
2   women and children; they exchange litter for food.
3   More people can get on quickly.
4   You can save time by buying your ticket beforehand, and buses have dedicated bus lanes.
5   the will to change, and the involvement of all the citizens
6   *Suggested answer:* Streets are now much cleaner because of the voluntary recycling exchange system. Moreover, public transport is far better, and initiatives introduced by the authorities have helped to reduce traffic jams. (*30 words*)

B   1D   2B   3A

C   1   to give up a hectic, high-earning lifestyle in favour of a low-income but more satisfying one
2   At this stage it is possible to take the final step into a new, simpler lifestyle.
3   They were working too hard to enjoy their hobbies. / They did not really enjoy the consumerist approach to life.
4   signed up for
5   He rents a floor of his old house from his daughter.
6   He thinks people are too self-indulgent and eat unnecessary amounts.
7   the New Road Map Foundation
8   Joe Dominguez and Vicki Robin
9   struck a chord
10   good use of money, good bargains, lack of show
11   the things they enjoy
12   *Suggested answer:* Downshifting involves spending more time on worthwhile activities in order to get the most satisfaction out of life. Usually people give up their stressful, high-income job in favour of a part-time one, or simply do voluntary work. 'Making do' instead of buying the latest consumer or fashion items is also important. (*51 words*)

# Unit 4

A   1   Yes: 'At first glance the village looked just the same.'
2   In the past: 'It seemed a waste, somehow.'
3   Moira has been locked up by someone, or at least appears isolated in her room. The Baron's ghost has appeared several times and attacked or killed two people already.
4   She is cold and also dreading the possible appearance of the Baron's ghost.
5   To Luxembourg, to visit her mother or other elderly female relative.
6   Both working, busy lifestyles, possibly too busy to talk.
7   a) worried, hard-working, caring   b) hard-working, exhausted   c) enthusiastic, careful

B (*These are suggested answers only – others may be appropriate.*)
  1  girlfriend and boyfriend?
  2  their relationship? breaking up? his personality problems?
  3  Probably Liz, as she is taking the initiative.
  4  a) tense, vulnerable, a worrier  b) self-centred, cool  c) American?
  5  Probably they always go to a certain seminar on Tuesdays.
  6  See you later.
  7–9  *need subjective answers.*

C  1  private investigator/detective
  2  whether the man has committed a crime or not
  3  She finds him attractive, but she knows he might be a criminal.
  4  No, because he looked at her while she was looking in her bag.
  5  a) She is enthusiastic and hard-working, perhaps a bit romantic.
      b) He is busy all day, moving around town. He is aware of fashion and likes good clothes.
  6  without anyone noticing
  7  They are probably employees, contacts or accomplices of the man she has been following, and have come to speak to her.
  8  The two men might give her a warning, threaten or kidnap her.

D  1  her flatmate Mariska, who failed to wake her up
  2  She's cross with them for letting the boss know she's arrived late, and for not supporting her when she needs their help.
  3  She respects Deepak, but thinks he makes too much fuss over unpunctuality.
  4  not seriously interested in work
  5  secretly went out
  6  No, because the sauce was 'unidentifiable' and there was 'absolutely zero' to watch on TV.
  7  give Mariska a stern warning
  8  romance ('love is in the air'), clothes ('ruined my new cream trousers'), and her appearance ('too fat', 'too many')

# Practice 2

A  1D  2B  3B  4C  5A  6D
B  1A  2B  3C  4D  5C  6D  7A

# Unit 5

B  *Suggested answers:* chocoholic, felt at home, ancient Mayan civilisation, Central America, sophisticated culture, chocolate, central role, a drink, a form of currency, cacao bean, three thousand years, a drink, most of that time

C  1  Australia
  2  mouth-watering, delicious
  3  Lizard Island
  4  Lady Elliott Island
  5  Heron Island
  6  Lizard Island
  7  Fraser Island

D  1  north-west India
  2  before 1500
  3  Egyptian
  4  Romany
  5  education and healthcare
  6  over 100,000

E 1 Dr Sally Ward
  2 none
  3 no more than one hour a day
  4 10 years
  5 Manchester

F 1 Siam, now known as Thailand
  2 63 years
  3 left and right
  4 They were shown to the public as an attraction.
  5 1874

# Unit 6

A 1C 2D 3E 4A 5B 6F 7H

B 1I 2A 3C 4B 5D 6H 7G 8J 9E 10F

C A 1I 2F 3I 4F 5I 6I 7F

  B 1F 2F 3F 4F 5I 6F 7I 8I 9F 10I

D 1 advice about fire, notice, formal
  2 message/information, note to flatmate, informal
  3 insurance, policy document, formal
  4 DVD player, instruction booklet, formal
  5 sandwiches, note to workmates, informal

E carbon monoxide poisoning/health warning, article/leaflet, formal

F crime, residents' newsletter, informal

G home improvements/insulation, email/note/letter to a friend, informal

# Practice 3

A growing herbs, magazine article, informal

B music, magazine article/autobiography, informal

C swimming, notice in hotel, formal

D money/property, legal document/will, formal

E 1 1995
  2 Finland
  3 plant stanols, derived from wood pulp
  4 It reduces people's cholesterol levels.
  5 formal

F 1 its great age and its huge size
  2 Why was it built? What is it?
  3 so that a person's spirit could survive death
  4 pharaoh
  5 formal

G 1 films
  2 advertisement
  3 informal

# Key

## Section 2

### Unit 7
1C  2B  3A  4D  5D  6A

### Unit 8
1C  2B  3C  4B  5D  6A  7A

### Unit 9
1B  2C  3C  4A  5C  6A  7B  8B

### Unit 10
1C  2B  3D  4C  5A  6A  7B  8D

### Unit 11
1D  2B  3C  4D  5A  6C  7B  8A

## Section 3

### Unit 12
1E  2G  3B  4C  5F  6A
a) infectious  b) ugly  c) dangerous  d) terrifying
e) eradicate  f) grant  g) exploit  h) remind

### Unit 13
1C  2H  3E  4F  5D  6G  7A

### Unit 14
1B  2H  3A  4G  5D  6E  7F
a) diagnose  b) chain-smoke  c) economise  d) settle in
e) die young  f) in addition to  g) take its/their toll  h) in debt

### Unit 15
1D  2H  3F  4C  5G  6E  7B

### Unit 16
1C  2E  3G  4D  5A  6F  7B
a) native  b) artistic  c) distinctive  d) manual
e) affection  f) masterpiece  g) legacy  h) poverty

## Section 4

### Unit 17
1B/F  2B/F  3D/E  4D/E  5F/H  6F/H  7D/F  8D/F  9A  10E  11D  12C/G  13C/G  14B  15F

### Unit 18
1C  2G  3A/H  4A/H  5D/F  6D/F  7H  8F  9E  10B/C  11B/C  12E  13A  14G  15D

### Unit 19
1H  2C  3B  4F  5H  6B/D  7B/D  8A/G  9A/G  10F  11E  12C/E  13C/E  14H  15A

### Unit 20
1A/E  2A/E  3B  4C  5E  6A/D  7A/D  8C  9A/B  10A/B  11D  12A  13B/C  14B/C  15B

### Unit 21
1E  2D  3A  4C  5B  6A  7B  8F  9A  10C  11F  12F  13C  14E  15C

## Section 5

### Test 1
#### Part 1
1B  2A  3C  4B  5D  6C  7C  8B

#### Part 2
9G  10H  11E  12D  13C  14A  15B

#### Part 3
16E  17C  18B  19E  29A/D  21A/D  22C  23B/D  24B/D  25D  26A  27E  28C  29B  30E

## Test 2
### Part 1
1C  2D  3A  4C  5B  6C  7A  8D

### Part 2
9B  10G  11A  12H  13E  14F  15D

### Part 3
16E  17B  18A  19E  20D  21A/C  22A/C  23B/E  24B/E  25E  26B  27E  28D  29A/E  30A/E


## Test 3
### Part 1
1D  2B  3A  4C  5B  6D  7A  8C

### Part 2
9F  10H  11B  12E  13G  14D  15C

### Part 3
16B  17A  18E  19C  20A  21E  22D  23B  24A  25B  26C  27E  28C  29B  30B


## Test 4
### Part 1
1A  2D  3A  4C  5B  6B  7C  8D

### Part 2
9E  10B  11G  12A  13H  14D  15F

### Part 3
16B  17C  18E  19A  20B  21D  22A  23D  24B  25E  26E  27B  28A  29C  30A